THE GOSPEL IN EXODUS

'CHRIST IS ALL'

THE GOSPEL IN EXODUS

★

HENRY LAW

THE BANNER OF TRUTH TRUST
78b Chiltern Street, London W1

First published 1855
First Banner of Truth Trust 1967

SET IN 11 ON 12 PT LINOTYPE GEORGIAN AND
PRINTED IN GREAT BRITAIN BY
HAZELL WATSON & VINEY LTD, AYLESBURY, BUCKS

CONTENTS

THE BURNING BUSH

*'He looked, and, behold, the Bush burned with fire, and the
Bush was not consumed.' Exod. 3.3*

Wondrous is the sight which here meets our view. It is a
Bush in flames, but not consumed. Destroying fire fails to
destroy. Perishable wood refuses to be fuel.

Reader, this surely is no new object to you. But know that
it abounds in lessons which your search cannot exhaust.

It must be so. The unsearchable riches of Jesus are in this
mine. He, who is the Wonder of Wonders, is the true Wonder of the Bush.

Reader, you must see Christ by faith, if ever you would
see God and enter heaven. You must know Christ in heart,
if ever you would know peace in conscience and hope in
death. Pray then the Holy Spirit that He would make the
blazing Bush to be a blaze of saving light within your soul.

The way to the burning Bush lies through an avenue of
instructive thoughts.

Moses is mercifully rescued from an early grave of waters.
Pharaoh's decree dooms to death. But Pharaoh's daughter
is the means of life. When God has purposes to work, He
can make foes his tools. The oppressor's court becomes the
refuge of the oppressed. The Hebrew child is caressed as an
Egyptian prince.

But the perils of the Nile are scarcely greater to the body,
than the perils of the palace to the soul. Worldly pomp is
very dazzling. Worldly luxury is very fascinating. Worldly
pleasures are very ensnaring. But there is an ark of safety in
the flood of vanities, as in the flood of waters. Moses is
neither dazzled, nor fascinated, nor ensnared. He looks
above, and sees a splendour far more bright. He deliberately
chooses scorn and affliction and loss and penury, with the

7

people of God. And he finds such scorn to be the truest honour – such affliction to be the purest joy – such loss to be the richest gain – such penury to be the most enduring wealth.

Reader, it is an important principle, that none can tread the world beneath their feet until they see a fairer world above their heads. When the Lord is set before you, your eyes are dim to lower objects. The beauty of the all-beauteous makes other loveliness unlovely.

Moses proves the mighty energy of soul-elevating, soul-purifying faith. This stirring principle turns his whole course from ease and pelf and self, into one stream of daring activities for God. He beholds with aching heart Israel's crushed tribes. He boldly presents himself to avenge their wrongs, and to erect the standard of their freedom. But what is the welcome which awaits him? Alas! he is thrust away with a rejecting taunt, 'Who made thee a prince and a judge over us?' Exod. 2.14.

Reader, your eyes are open to such pitiable folly. You sigh over a serfdom, which is content to do a tyrant's bidding, rather than defy a tyrant's rage. But such may be your own case. The Gospel, like Moses, approaches men. It tells them that they grind in Satan's prison-house. It calls them to arise from the dust, to lift up the head, to burst the fetters, to dare to be free. It shows them Jesus, the Captain of Salvation, inviting them to the banner of His cross. It assures them that this Leader never lost a battle – and never lost a man. It beseeches them to cast off the filthy fetters, and to stride boldly towards the sparkling crown. What answer is returned? Alas! multitudes hate the voice which would arouse them. They hug the bonds which bind them to perdition's cell. They little think how soon each link in that chain will become a deathless scorpion and a quenchless flame.

'Then fled Moses at this saying.' Acts 7.29. Reader, take

heed. The decree may issue, he 'is joined to idols; let him alone.' Hos. 4.17. An unwelcomed Saviour may depart for ever. The wings of love may fly away in judgment.

He was hid as a stranger in the land of Midian forty years. But the God who was his shield in the crowd, was his sun in the desert. It is sad, that the Lord's servant must be earth's outcast. But it is sweet to see how heavenly wisdom can make the hardest usage to yield our choicest blessings. The sweetest honey is from the stony rock. There was work for Moses which required lamb-like meekness with lion-like resolve. He must be calm as ocean when it sleeps: firm as the rock which smiles at storms. These are the lessons of tribulation's school: – therefore, in tribulation he must be schooled. Metal becomes pure by long process in the furnace. The wisdom which is profitable in the busy haunts of busy men, grows in retirement's still shade. In the seclusion of Arabia, Paul drinks calmly of truth's fount. In the wilds of Midian, Moses sits at the feet of God.

At last the appointed time of rescue came. God's works are the reflection of decrees ordained of old. When His purposes were ripe, a marvel startles the shepherd-prophet. A Bush blazes before him, each branch, each fibre reddened in the flame. But neither branch nor fibre received hurt. The brittle wood waved an uninjured head. Well might Moses wonder. But wonder deepened into awe, when from the Bush a voice was heard, even the voice of God.

Reader, it becomes us now to ask, what is the Gospel of the burning Bush? Jesus Himself appears in His person, suffering, and all-resisting might.

His person – He is God, and yet He stoops to be made man. He is man, and yet He continues to be God for ever. Withdraw the Godhead, and His blood cannot atone. Withdraw the manhood, and no blood remains. The union gives a Saviour able, and a Saviour meet. Look to the Bush. It shows this very union. The wood denotes the poor and feeble

9

produce of earth. It exhibits the 'tender plant' – the 'root out of a dry ground.' But it holds God as its inmate. The voice out of its midst proclaims, Your God is here.

His sufferings – Fire wraps the Bush. No clearer image can depict the hot assaults of wrath. The life of Jesus knew these well. It was one struggle with keen anguish. Earth was a thorny path. Hell shot its every shaft. Heaven darkened with the horrors of its frowns. All the fierce pains which infinite displeasure could inflict, made Him their prey. He wrung out all, which all the ransomed would have tasted, if hell-agonies had been their doom for ever.

His all-resisting might – In vain the fire assailed the bush. It stood unharmed. So every blow recoiled from Jesus. Sustained by His indwelling Deity, He trod all foes beneath His feet. He burst the bands of death. He shivered the grave's gates. He stood victorious on the ruins of hell's empire. He mounted in triumph to the heaven of heavens.

We have next an undoubted figure of the whole family of faith. Persecutions and trials are the fire, which assails them with ceaseless fury. But still they thrive and strengthen and bud and blossom and flourish. How can it be? Deity indwells them. And where Deity resides there must be undecaying life.

The Church's story is a mirror of this truth. How often do we see it as a tiny bark tossed in engulfing waves. The powers of the mighty, the craft of the subtle, the rage of the frantic, have seized it with terrific grasp. Evil men have done their worst: evil spirits have aimed blows: evil fiends have put forth spite. Surely the fragile Bush must sink in ruin. But no! It defies all foes. It stands, and ever will stand, verdant and fragrant and fruitful.

But the power of resistance is not its own. The Lord is in the midst. He has chosen it as His abode for ever. They are precious tidings. 'In the midst of the seven candlesticks is one like unto the Son of man.' Rev. 1.13.

It is true that Jesus, as God, holds all space within His hand. 'His centre is everywhere, His circumference is no-where.' But still the Church is the chosen home of His un-bounded love. Here His all-protecting might, His all-pre-serving care, His full delights, repose. He received it from His Father as His spouse – His jewels – His peculiar treasure – His portion – the fulness of His body – the completeness of His mediatorial glory. He is engaged to seat it, as an un-diminished family, before the throne. If one member be injured, Christ is marred; if one be absent, Christ is maimed. Hence He is ever with it – all heart to love – all eye to watch – all hand to help – all wisdom to direct – all power to beat back foes. Let, then, the fire rage. It must be mightier than Almightiness before the Bush can droop to nothingness.

Do these lines meet the eye of one who plots and strives against Zion's weal? Vain man, forbear! The promise ever lives, 'Lo! I am with you alway.' Can you tear the sun from its high seat? Can you beat back ocean with a feather? Can you bind the lightning with a straw? Such task were easier than to pluck Jesus from the Bush. Because He lives there, His people shall live also.

Here, too, another mystery is solved. Grace seems but a tender plant in the believer's heart. It has to contend with nipping frosts and desolating storms. Satan's rage burns hot against it. The world brings fuel upon fuel to consume it. The flesh blows fiercely to fan the flame. But grace still thrives. Its roots spread. Its branches rise. Its fruit ripens. Why? Christ walks within His garden – a guardian-God. His hand sowed each seed. The dew of His favour nourishes it. The smile of His love matures it. Hence it overtops all fiery foes, and lifts its head towards heaven.

Believer, think much of the 'goodwill of Him that dwelt in the Bush.' Deut. 33.16. Fears then will flee away. If you stood alone, it would be presumption to hope. Because you are not alone, it is offence to tremble.

Look back. Many conflicts are behind, and yet you live. How is it? You reply with Paul, 'The Lord stood with me and strengthened me.' 'The Bush burned with fire, and the Bush was not consumed.' Your present fight is hot. But you hear a much-loved voice, 'Fear thou not, for I am with thee.' 'The Bush burns with fire, and the Bush is not consumed.' You look onward. The horizon is dark with clouds of tribulation. But the same voice cheers, 'Fear not': 'when thou walkest through the fire, thou shalt not be burned.' The captive youths, a cloud of witnesses, an army of blessed martyrs, wave you forward. They tell that persecuting flames may be despoiled of all their sting. Rejoice then. The Bush shall burn with fire, but it shall not be consumed.

Reader, pause here, and search your conscience. Is your body a temple of Jesus Christ, through the Spirit? Is Christ dwelling in your heart by faith? Is Christ in you, the hope of glory? If it be not so, touch not the comfort of the burning Bush. Remember, there are thorns and briers, 'whose end is to be burned.' No Saviour saves them. Tares must be bound in bundles for wrath's full-heated furnace. A terrible voice wails from the region of the lost, 'I am tormented in this flame.' 'The day cometh that shall burn as an oven: and all the proud, yea, and all that do wickedly, shall be stubble.' Mal. 4.1. 'The smoke of their torment ascendeth up for ever and ever.' Rev. 14.11.

Reader, here are words by which, through grace, you may be saved. Turn not away to everlasting burnings. If you are so mad, this warning will lie, as a hot coal, upon your soul for ever.

'I AM THAT I AM'

'I am that I am.' Exod. 3.14

The believer is called to wayfaring and warfaring struggles. He has to bear a daily cross and to fight a daily fight. But in every hour of need a sure support is near. Behold Moses. The ground which he must tread is very slippery. The hill of his difficulties is very steep. A foe opposes every step. But a staff and a sword are provided for him in the name of his guiding and protecting Lord. 'I AM THAT I AM.' On this he can lean the whole burden of his cares, and fears, and pains. By this he can scatter kings as dust. This stay is still the same, ever mighty, ever near. The feeblest pilgrim may grasp it by the hand of faith. And whosoever grasps it is 'as mount Zion, which cannot be removed, but abideth for ever.'

'I AM THAT I AM.' Such is the voice from the burning bush. The Speaker, then, is hid in no mask of mystery. It is the Angel of the everlasting Covenant. It is the great Redeemer. He would establish His people on the firm rock of comfort. Therefore with trumpet-tongue He thus assures them that all the majesty, all the supremacy, all the glory of absolute and essential Deity, are His inherent right.

O my soul, into what a speck must poor man dwindle before such greatness! The limits of the mind cannot scan it. The arms of the heart cannot embrace it. Words are mere skeletons before it. Intellect would fain on eagle's wing fly around the ever-widening circle. But vain is the effort. Its height is on heaven's summit. What mortal arm can reach it? It is as space which has no bounds. What human line can measure it? Our mortal eyes pierce not unlimited expanse. Our scales weigh not the mountains. Our vessels measure not the ocean's depths. So our faculties are too short to probe the immensities of God. To grasp divine essence requires divine largeness. 'I AM THAT I AM' alone can read the volume of that title.

Shall we then repine? What! repine because our God is so great? Where is the subject who frets because he cannot count his prince's treasures? Let us rather bow our heads in pious adoration. Let us rather give thanks that a mine is open in which the very dust is gold. Let us rather humble ourselves, that we are so slow and careless to gather up the manna of rich truth which falls at the tent-door. Let us rather pray the Spirit to illumine more clearly the written page. Let us rather long for the day when every cloud which veils our God shall brighten into perfect light; and when His people 'shall be like Him, for they shall see Him as He is.'

Come then, and with such loving teachableness let us take our seat beside this sea of truth, and strive with reverence to touch the spray which sparkles on the shore.

'I AM THAT I AM.' Here the first sound is eternity. Jesus, as God, here puts on eternity as His robe. He knows no past. He knows no future. He lives unmoved in one unmoving present. He stretches through all the ages which are gone and which are yet to come. His only bounds are immeasurable boundlessness. Ere time was born, He is 'I AM THAT I AM.' When time shall have expired, He still is 'I AM THAT I AM.' If there had been the moment when His being dawned, His name would be, 'I am what I was not.' If there could be a moment when His being must have end, His name would be, 'I am what I shall not be.' But He is, 'I AM THAT I AM.' Thus He treads first and last beneath His feet. He sits on the unbroken circumference of existence, as He who ever was, and ever is, and ever shall be. Let thought fly back, until in weariness it faint; let it look onward until all vision fail; it ever finds Him the same 'I AM.'

Reader, look down now from this astounding glory and fix your eye on Bethlehem's manger. A lowly Babe lies in the lowly cradle of a lowly town, the offspring of a lowly mother. Look again. That child is the eternal 'I AM.' He whose Deity never had birth, is born 'the woman's Seed.' He, whom no infinitudes can hold, is contained within Infant's age, and Infant's form. He, who never began to be, as God, here begins to be, as man. And can it be, that the great 'I AM THAT I AM' shrinks into our flesh, and is little upon our earth, as one newborn of yesterday? It is so. The Lord promised it. Prophets foretold it. Types prefigured it. An angel announces it. Heaven rings with rapture at it. Faith sees it. The redeemed rejoice in it.

But wherefore is this wonder of wonders? Wherefore is eternity's Lord a Child of time? He thus stoops, that He may save poor wretched sinners such as we are. Could He not do so by His will or by His word? Ah! no. He willed, and all things were. He speaks, and all obey. But he must die, as man, that a lost soul may live. To rescue from one stain of sin, the Eternal must take the sinner's place, and bear sin's curse and pay sin's debt, and suffer sin's penalty, and wash out sin's filth, and atone for sin's malignity. 'I AM THAT I AM' alone could do this. 'I AM THAT I AM' alone has done it.

What self-denial, what self-abasement, what self-emptying is here! Surely, royalty in rags, angels in cells, is no descent compared to Deity in flesh! But mighty love moves Jesus to despise all shame, and to lie low in misery's lowest mire. Through ages past His 'delights were with the sons of men.' Prov. 8.31. Eternity to come is but a void, unless his people share His glory. Therefore He humbles Himself to earth, that specks of earth may rise to heaven's immortality. Believer, you joy in prospect of thus living with Him for ever. But wherefore is there full rapture in the thought? Do not you feel that the crowning ecstasy is in this? Eternity

15

will afford you time to gaze with steady look on a Saviour's glories, to sing with unwearied hymn a Saviour's praise, to bless with perpetual blessing a Saviour's name, and to learn with ever-expanding knowledge a Saviour's worth.

There is another note in this loud chorus of truth, which is especial sweetness to the believer's ear. It tells melodiously that Jesus cannot change. He is as constant as He is great. As surely as He ever lives, so surely He ever lives the same. He is one expanse of never-varying oneness. He sits on the calm throne of eternal serenity.

Change is the defect of things below: for things below are all defective. Immutability reigns above: for immutability is perfection's essence. Our brightest morn oft ends in storm. Summer's radiance gives place to winter's gloom. The smiling flower soon lies withered. The babbling brook is soon a parched-up channel. The friend who smiled, smiles no more friendly welcomes. Bereavement weeps where once the family beamed with domestic joy. Gardens wither into deserts. Babylons crumble into unsightly ruins. On all things a sad inscription writes 'fleeting – transient – vanishing.' Time flaps a ceaseless wing, and from the wings decay and death drop down. 'I AM THAT I AM' sits high above all this. He is 'the same yesterday, and to-day, and for ever.'

The unchangeableness of Jesus is the unchangeableness of His attributes. Each shines brightly in this bright mirror. But a rapid glance at His love and power must suffice.

His love is in perpetual bloom. It is always in summer-tide. The roots are deeply buried in Himself; therefore the branches cannot fade. Believer, drink hourly of this cup of joy. Suffer not Satan to infuse a poisonous doubt. Christ loved you largely when, in the councils of eternity, He received you into His heart. He loved you truly when, in the fulness of time, He took upon Himself your curse, and drained your hell-deep dues. He loved you tenderly when He showed you, by the Spirit, His hands and His feet, and

16

whispered to you that you were His. He loves you faithfully while He ceases not to intercede in your behalf, and to scatter blessings on your person and your soul. He will love you intensely in heaven when you are manifested as His purchase and crowned as His bride. To each enquiry – has He loved? does He love? and will He love? – the one reply is, 'I AM THAT I AM.'

Do not raise the objection, if He thus loves, why am I thus? why is my path so rugged, and my heart like flint? You will soon know that your bitterest trials and your sorest pains are sure tokens of His love. The father corrects because he loves. In anxious care the physician deeply probes the wounds. Thus Jesus makes earth hard, that you may long for heaven's holy rest. He shows you your self-vileness that you may prize His cleansing blood. He suffers you to stumble that you may cleave more closely to His side. He makes the world a blank that you may seek all comfort in Himself. If He seem to change, it is that you may change. He hides His face, that you may look towards Him. He is silent, that you may cry more loudly. His desertion prevents your desertion. He saves from real hell, by casting into seeming hell. But love fails not. All His dealings are its everflowing, overflowing tide. On each the eye of faith can read, 'I AM THAT I AM.'

Power goes hand in hand with love. They co-exist and co-endure. It was a mighty voice which said, 'Be' – and all things were. It was a mighty hand which framed this so wondrous universe. It is a mighty arm which turns the wheel of providence. This power still is, and ever will be, what it always has been. No age enfeebles, and no use exhausts it. This is the Church's rock. The Bible, blazing with its exploits, encourages the 'worm Jacob' to 'be strong in the Lord, and in the power of His might.' He can still bid the seas of difficulty to recede. He can cause hurricanes and tempests to cease. He can make straight the crooked paths of evil. He can level the mountains of high-towering corruption. He can stop the lion-mouth of persecution. He can quench the scorching flames of every lust. In the face of all Goliaths, He cheers His followers to victory, under the banner of 'I AM THAT I AM.'

Reader, these thoughts scarce touch the boundary line of the shadow of this glorious name. But surely they show the blessedness of those who, guided by the Spirit, repose beneath the wings of Jesus. 'The eternal God is thy refuge and underneath are the everlasting arms.' Deut. 33.27. 'I AM THAT I AM' must perish or must change, before their names can be cast from His heart. Some greater power must arise, before they can be plucked from His tight-grasping hand. The bare idea is folly. Happy flock! 'I AM THAT I AM' loves them, and they are loved: – calls them, and they follow Him: sanctifies them, and they are sanctified: – blesses them, and they are blessed: – gives them life, and they live: – gives them glory, and they are glorified.

But perhaps it is your wretched case to live unsprinkled by His saving blood. Will you die thus? What, thus appear before His great white throne? His truth condemns you – and it cannot change. His wrath burns hot against you – and it cannot relent. His power has commission to destroy you – and it cannot be withstood. 'I AM THAT I AM' becomes an idle fable, if truth and wrath and power war not eternally with sin. And can they war and not prevail?

Believer, the eternity and unchangeableness of 'I AM THAT I AM' makes heaven to be heaven for ever. Sinner, the eternity and unchangeableness of 'I AM THAT I AM' makes hell to be hell for ever.

THE PASSOVER

These words send us back to the last night of Israel's bondage in the land of Egypt. The captives had suffered much and long. The iron furnace had been heated by unpitying hate and by unsparing hands. But God, in His high council, had decreed that a morn of deliverance should dawn. The appointed hour came. No power can now detain. Mad opposition becomes weak. The chosen people must go free.

Believer, stay your soul on the rock of the promises. They are as immovable as He who speaks them. At the set moment you shall march in triumph to your Canaan.

Let us, in thought, intermingle in the solemn scene. It was a night black in dismays, terrible in judgments, wild in affrights, keen in anguish. Throughout the whole of Egypt's empire every house was woe, every face was horror, every heart was misery. Death forced all doors. Each eldest child was a lifeless corpse. There was no exception. The monarch and the slave alike bewailed, in bitter cry, their first-born's sudden and untimely slaughter.

It was a night memorable, too, in sweet displays of tender love. Israel's favoured sons were all assembled. But neither death nor fear was in their dwellings. They were equipped for departure from all cruelties and pains. They were feasting at a heaven-appointed board. They were rejoicing in a Gospel ordinance. They were partaking of a lamb slain. This exhibited, in loudly-speaking rites, all the certainties and all the mercies of spiritual redemption. They realized present escape. They looked forward to future safety. They had much in hand. They had more in view.

Reader, let us with joy join these joyous companies. And may the Christ-revealing Spirit show Christ to us, as the substance and truth and glory of the spread feast!

God Himself selects the offering. His voice says, 'They shall take to them every man a lamb.' Ex. 12.3. Thus Jesus is appointed by heavenly wisdom to be the one redeeming sacrifice. An elected Saviour is the strong foundation of salvation's pyramid. Blessed provision of our blessing God! Whither could we turn, if bidden to find a guilt-removing victim? But grace meets every want. Hearken to the sure tidings, 'Behold my servant, whom I uphold: mine elect, in whom my soul delighteth.' Is. 42.1.

Reader, God's only begotten Son is God's only appointed Redeemer. He only is called to bear His people's sins. For He only can sustain such load. He only is sent to make atonement. For He only has worthy blood to shed. He only is commissioned to bring in reconciliation. For He only can covenant with God. Obey God. Present Jesus in the arms of faith. Then your crimson stain is whiter than snow. Your soul is saved. Reject Him, and there remains no more sacrifice for sins.

The lamb must be a male of the earliest age (v. 5.). These are signs of vigour in unbroken perfection. Truly He who is to save must be mighty in strength. For think what mighty hindrances oppose. Whose arm can hold back the descending arm of divine wrath? Whose shoulder can sustain the weight of countless sins? Whose force can close hell? Whose power can open heaven? Whose prowess can trample down satanic rage, satanic spirits, and satanic men? In none but Jesus can such sufficiency be found. In Him it abounds to the overflowing of almightiness. The Father's voice proclaims, 'I have laid help upon one that is mighty.' Ps.89.19. The pledge is given, 'He shall send them a Saviour, and a great one.' Is. 19.20. The fulfilment is in Jesus, 'The great God and our Saviour.' Tit. 2.13. He is the Lamb in all the energy of perfect strength.

The Lamb must be 'without blemish.' (v. 5.). Jesus, while man below, was pure as God in heaven's brightness. Sin strove in vain to soil Him. Foul temptations thickly fell, but left Him spotless as the light of day. The Father's eye, which cannot look upon uncleanness, delighted in Him as the clear mirror of His own glory. In Him, human nature shone in the lustre of divine holiness. In Him was sinlessness which could atone for sin. In Him was righteousness which satisfied the law.

The lamb must be set apart for four days. (v. 6.). Thus in heaven, through eternal days, Jehovah's eye inspected Jesus, as the fore-ordained expiation for the foreseen evil. Thus on earth, through the days preceding the cross, He was tested by every judge: and thus, universal consent crowned Him with the crown of untarnished blamelessness. Even Satan, speaking by blood-guilty lips, proclaimed that there was no fault in Him. John 19.6.

The lamb must be slain by the whole assembly of the congregation (v. 6.). Not one voice was silent, when the awful cry went forth, 'Crucify Him, crucify Him.' Believer, not one sin of all your life was absent, when He was dragged to the cross. All your transgressions strained the cords. They concurred to drive in the nails, and to make deep the wounds. Your iniquities brought in that death. That death brings in your life.

The blood must be sprinkled on the lintel, and on the doorposts of each dwelling. (v. 7.). The blood shed must be used. It must be openly exhibited as a distinguishing sign. If the destroyer find the preserving mark, the foot of vengeance must pass over. If there be no shield of blood, the arrows of death must do their work. Reader, the Gospel moves poor sinners to appropriating efforts. Christ is uplifted, that eyes may look to Him. He is an open refuge, that feet may fly to Him. His blood flowed, that it may be taken by the hand of faith. Do you live a blood-besprinkled life? Is your soul at all times fresh dripping from this stream? If so, you safely dwell beneath salvation's wings. Justice cannot drag you to execution. The curse cannot blight you. The law cannot condemn you. Vengeance cannot slay you. The blood upon you cries: Away, stand back, no foe can touch, where I protect. But are you thus marked as Christ's? If not, arise speedily and flee unto the wounded Lamb. The day is far spent; the night of ruin is at hand. The destroyer is at your heels. Each house unmarked was a house unspared. Each soul unwashed will be a soul undone. An applied remedy alone can heal.

Not one drop stained the floor. The blood of Jesus is the most precious thing in heaven and in earth. The Father honours it with all heaven's honours. The saints in light praise it with all heaven's praises. The saints on earth joy in it with all heart's rapture. Satan flees before it. Shall godless men treat it with rejecting scorn? Let them beware: on the heart it is a seal of life: beneath the feet it is the stamp of hell.

The flesh must be roast with fire. (v. 8.). We have here the keenest image of the keenest torture. The pain of pains is to be slowly devoured by the scorching flames. But this is a faint image of what Jesus verily endured. O my soul, deal closely with the sufferings of your suffering Lamb. Let the amazing facts be the very fibres of your constant thought. Daily visit the garden. Hourly study the cross. What is the sight, what are the sounds, which there confront you? The God-man Jesus lies crushed to the earth. He bends beneath a weight of woe. The saddest groans proclaim the writhings of a tortured soul. Each pore weeps blood. Agony could not more agonize. A piteous cry confesses that the black horrors of desertion blackened around Him. These marks of extremest anguish have clear meaning. The Passover is roast with fire.

Believer, Jesus is tormented in your stead. All the wrath which all your sins deserved is outpoured on Him. The vengeance of God descends in all its fury. The curse of the law exacts its utmost. The flames of hell tightly grasp Him. He endures the very miseries which all His people must have endured if they had wailed for ever in the lake of fire. Faith sees it and exclaims: I live, for Jesus died. I cannot suffer. Jesus has exhausted all. Wrath cannot touch me, because it has touched Him.

Each inmate of the house must feed upon the lamb (v. 8.). So every one who would be saved must verily partake of Christ. To hear of Him, to touch the emblems of His dying love, to know His merits, to commend His worth, will profit little. Faith takes Christ, Christ Himself, as its own. It makes Him the very juice and substance of the inner man. Here is the believer's never-ending banquet. He feasts on Christ now. He will feast with Christ for ever.

A bone of the lamb may not be broken. (v. 46.). Jesus indeed was hardly used. But no wounds marred the proportion of His stature. They weakened not the pillars of His strength. He lives all-vigorous in salvation's might. He stands the unbroken, the unblemished column of His people's hopes. The marvellous fulfilment, too, of this command, proves Jesus of Nazareth to be the true Passover of God. When the soldiers 'came to Jesus and saw that He was dead already, they brake not His legs.' John 19.33. The unwitting heathen unwittingly accomplished the Jewish type. Infidelity, what can you reply? Know, that as no ignorance is like yours, so no ruin will be like yours.

The lamb must be eaten with bitter herbs and unleavened bread. (v. 8.). These requirements shadow out the combined graces of penitence and sincerity. Reader, do you boast of hope in Christ? It only dwells in a heart ground to powder under a sense of sin. Tears are the magnifying medium through which the cross attracts. Faith has no root in rocky soil. It only blossoms in the moist garden of a weeping spirit. They come in sorrow's sackcloth who receive Christ's justifying robe.

Do you boast that Christ is your feast? Where is your unleavened bread? Sin loved, sin cherished, sin retained, turns heaven's food into hell's poison. A searching eye comes in to see the guests. Leaven in their hands, leaven in their mouths, leaven in their hearts, is a fatal mark. They must go away to the cell of hypocrites.

The lamb must be eaten in the attitude of haste, and with equipment for departure. (v. 11.). The loins must be girded. The feet must be shod. The hands must hold the staff. Here is the believer waiting for his summons, with wings expanded towards his far-off home. Earth's ties are all severed. Anchors are weighed. The eye is strained for the signal, 'Come up hither.' Reader, are you thus ready? It is miserable to have ought to do, when doing-time is past. He is a foolish servant who has to seek the key when his Lord knocks. He is a poor advocate, who has to find a plea when he is called to plead. When death comes, have nothing to do, but just to die.

Believer, may you hear, in these poor lines, the Spirit calling you to this Gospel feast. It is His voice, 'Christ our Passover is sacrificed for us: therefore let us keep the feast; not with the old leaven, neither with the leaven of malice and wickedness: but with the unleavened bread of sincerity and truth.' 1 Cor. 5.7, 8. I deeply feel that without His light, His grace, His power, we cannot see or know or love or serve or glorify our Lord. But may He vouchsafe to open our eyes, that we may behold the rich plenteousness of our paschal-board! May He show us the glories of Jesus, as the Lamb slain! May He enable us to receive Him as our All! May He fill our hearts with the longing prayer: 'Come, Lord Jesus, come quickly.'

REDEMPTION

'All the first-born of man among thy children shalt thou redeem.'
Exod. 13.13

If there be a theme which claims incessant thought, it is Redemption. Job's sweetest word is, 'I know that my Redeemer liveth.' Job. 19.25. Heaven is a pyramid of redeemed souls. The melody of eternal harps is, 'Thou wast slain, and hast redeemed us to God by Thy blood.' Rev. 5.9.

Reader, study, then, I pray you, Redemption more and more. Explore its need, its plan, its worth, its end. Without this knowledge your soul is dark, your heart is cold, faith has no sure resting-place, hope has no anchor, love has no kindling flame, service has no constraining motive. Except this stream flow in a deep channel, the Bible is the mocking course of a summer brook.

It is the Spirit's will that we should clearly see and tightly grasp this subject. He announces it in plainest terms. He embodies it in distinct images. He paints it in vivid types. He predicts it in prophetic song. He exhibits it in holy rites. Thus in the earliest pages of Israel's story an ordinance stands forward, which surely is designed to cast a flood of revealing rays on the main features of redeeming work.

The first-fruits of man's race throughout Egypt's empire are cut down by one fell swoop. But in the blood-marked dwellings no parent weeps, no offspring bleeds. A seed is spared. But He who spares it claims it as His own. The Lord speaks unto Moses, saying, 'Sanctify unto me all the first-born.' Exod. 13.2. They are doubly His. He created; He preserved.

But tender mercy here finds an opening to show a smiling face. Ransom is decreed. If a fit sum, according to the balance of the sanctuary, be paid, the claim shall be remitted, the forfeited progeny shall be free. Num. 3.47.

Such is the rite. It has especial value, because it gives a clue to the grand lesson of the Gospel-school. We here are taught the meaning of Redemption. It is recovery on account of payment made. A Redeemer receives again, only because He fills the scales with satisfying sums.

Reader, now lift aloft this torch. It helps you to discern the realities and immensities of the Redemption which is effected by the Lord. Sinners are the lost property. Souls are the captive heritage. Christ regains them at the price of His most precious blood. Ponder the breadth and length of this great fact. Mark the vile thraldom into which sin brought our race. It spoiled us all of spiritual liberty. It dragged us into the lowest cell of a dark prison-house. It placed Satan as the stern jailer of a guilt-enfettered world. From the day in which Adam touched the forbidden fruit, each child is born a captive, because he is born in sin. External circumstance may differ. But it changes not internal state. The high, the low, the rich, the poor, lie in one base level of sin-grasped, sin-sold misery. The whole family breathe their first breath, as common slaves in common slavery.

Not only spiritual liberty is lost, but spiritual life is slain. No slave of sin is conscious of his abject state. There is no loathing of the loathsome jail. There is no longing to reach holier ground. There is no panting for a purer clime.

But try to suppose a case which cannot be. Let the heart wish against the heart's desire. Let corruption sigh to burst corruption's bond. Where can one gleam of hope be found? Will tears or cries induce the jailer to relent? Can his hatred cease to hate? Can his malice melt to love? Can rocks dissolve to softness? Such things might be. But Satan must be Satan still. His being is to revel in our woe.

But can no striving strength beat down the subjugating

foe? Alas! Feebleness is a feeble word to paint our power when compared with his. Self cannot rescue self; nor man deliver man.

But cannot angels render aid? We may conceive that they look down in tender pity. But pity is not power. A yearning heart is not an arm of might. Let all the hosts of heaven fly forward to your help. How can they force the prison-walls which sin has raised? Captivity must remain, except Omnipotence arise to help.

Reader, now look to Jesus. All hope centres in Him. His gracious eye surveys a captive world. Within sin's walls He sees the bride, from all eternity beloved – the portion which the Heavenly Father gave Him – the jewels which are to be His crown for ever – the sheep whom He is pledged to tend – the children whose names are written on His heart – the heritage which was His delight before the worlds were made. He beholds them vile, in iniquity's vile rags – wretched to the last length of wretchedness – dark in the blackest night of hopelessness – trembling on the brink of uttermost perdition. He beholds them in this mire. He beholds them such, and yet He loves them.

Can He love and not seek their rescue? Can He live if they die? Can He rejoice if they wail? Can He reign if they perish? Can He shine in glory if they glare in hell?

It cannot be. They are His property by His Father's gift. They are the fulness of His mystic body. He must redeem them. But how? Suppose Him suppliant at the dungeon-gate. Can He by word of strong entreaty gain their freedom? No! Holy attributes of God forbid. A book appears against them, written throughout with countless charges, and exhibiting countless debts. Each debt is a roll of infinite extent. Can He pay all? He knows that in the boundlessness of His Deity He has strength to endure the penalty, and resources to wipe out the debt. Will He hesitate? Oh no! love constrains Him, pity moves Him; mercy urges

Him; the eternal covenant compels Him. To the extent of infinity He will suffer, if only by the infinity of His sufferings His people can be free. So He takes Redemption into His hands.

And will He verily accomplish it? O my soul, draw near and see. In the fulness of time, He comes flying on the wings of redeeming grace, striding in the might of redeeming power, clad in the armour of redeeming prowess, wearing on His brow Redemption's helmet, bearing in His hands Redemption's price.

Proceed with Him to the work. Enter with Him into the garden. Take your station beside His cross. He presents Himself to redeem. He draws near to endure His people's pains, to pay their wretched owings. The penalty of each sin is everlasting curse. Must this descend upon the sinless Surety? It must. It does. Holy wrath cannot spare. Holy Truth cannot unsay its word. The sinner's soul must die. All the agonies of never-ending dying must be borne. Jesus sustains, until Justice can inflict no more.

So, too, each debt is fully cancelled. The scales of heaven are brought forth. In the one there is the weight of iniquities, which would weigh worlds upon worlds into the lowest dust. Into the other Jesus casts His blood as counter-payment. The value infinitely exceeds. Justice exclaims, Release those souls, they have paid to the last mite. Jehovah issues His mighty mandate concerning each, 'Deliver him from going down to the pit; I have found a ransom.' Job 33.24. What now can Satan do? His rage, his malice, and his hate, are impotent to harm. The blood has satisfied all claims. The death has slain all foes. The cross has silenced each accusing voice. The portals can no more be barred. The chains are shivered. The prisoners are free. The captives are redeemed.

Who now presents a charge? Who now can urge a claim? Christ's death is super-abounding Redemption-price. O my soul, live reading those letters of love, which brightly shine around the cross. It is written, 'In whom we have Redemption through His blood, the forgiveness of sins, according to the riches of His grace.' Eph. 1.7.

Believer, you are purchased by this inestimable price. Know, then, what blessedness is yours. You are for ever free from all hell misery. Multitudes must reap the harvest which sin sows, in anguish never-ending. But avenging wrath cannot touch you. The gnawing worm cannot prey on you. The Redeemer has ransomed you. Rejoice, and give Him praise.

The wicked will soon be bound, body and soul, in bundles for the endless burning. Oh! the woe to be for ever linked with foul fiends – to be for ever hearing from their parched lips the execrating wail of hatred and despair! But you are safe. The Redeemer has ransomed you. Rejoice, and give Him praise.

How many pass their pilgrim-days in the vile service of this world's prince! He drives them at his will to every godless word and work. They drink the gall of disappointment, vexation, discontent, and terrible foreboding. But He who redeemed your life from destruction crowns you with loving-kindness and tender mercies. You have peace which passes all understanding – joys which are the earnest of Paradise – and hope which enters now within the veil of heaven. Rejoice, and give Him praise.

Many tremble at the approach of death. They know, that it will snap the thread of earthly being, and plunge them into agony's abyss. They hate life, because it ends in dying. They hate dying, because it ends their hopeless hopes. But death's features have no frown for you. It comes as a welcome friend to open the cage-door of the flesh, that the rejoicing spirit may fly swift to the Redeemer's breast.

The slaves of Satan dread the grave. They are conscious that it cannot detain the body long. Their dust must live again. The tabernacle in which they sinned must be the tabernacle in which they receive sin's wages. But your ears of faith have heard the Conqueror's shout, 'I will ransom them from the power of the grave. I will redeem them from death.' Hos. 13.14. The archangel's voice will soon awake the slumbering clay, and then it will put on the glorious robes of immortality, and shine forth in beauty, bright as His beauty, and in perfections fitted for the Eternal's throne.

Believer, hell only can draw up the murky veil, and fully show the miseries from which you are snatched by Christ. The resurrection morn, the nightless day alone can manifest your blood-bought blessing.

But hark! the Spirit speaks a word of wholesome warning. Redeemed ones are no more their own. 'Ye are bought with a price: therefore glorify God in your body, and in your spirit, which are God's.' 1 Cor. 6.20. Your time is redeemed; use it as a consecrated talent in His cause. Your minds are redeemed; employ them to learn His truth and, to meditate on His ways. Thus make them armouries of holy weapons. Your eyes are redeemed; let them not look on vanity; close them on all sights and books of folly. Your feet are redeemed; let them trample on the world, and climb the upward hill of Zion, and bear you onward in the march of Christian zeal. Your tongues are redeemed; let them only sound His praise, and testify to His love, and call sinners to His cross. Your hearts are redeemed; let them love Him wholly, and have no seat for rivals. A redeemed flock should live in Redemption's pastures. The Redeemer's freedmen should evidence that they are called to holy liberty, and that their holy liberty is holy service. The chain of sin is broken. The chain of love now holds them.

THE PILLAR

'The Lord went before them by day in a pillar of a cloud to lead them the way; and by night in a pillar of fire, to give them light; to go by day and night.' Exod. 13.21

The children of Israel are about to tread an unknown path. A desert is before them, wide and waste and trackless. They have no chart to show the way. There are no friendly lips to counsel or to warn. They must proceed, and yet they fear to stir.

This is a common need. Perhaps you, who read, discern your very case. You have left Egypt. The hated bonds are burst. But Canaan's rest is far away. An intervening wilderness extends. Hence the sigh rises in your breast, Oh! that some guide were near! How can the distant end be safely reached?

Israel's story gives the glad reply. Were they allowed to wander without beckoning succour? Oh! no. Whose hand, then, waved them forward? Did the Lord send some natives of the waste to teach where the paths were safe? No! Did He inspire their ruler's mind with instinct of the untrodden land? No! He comes Himself. He stoops to take the office of their guide.

But by what method is His directing aid made clear? A visible form, which every eye might see, reveals the wondrous guide. A pillar descends, and rests upon the camp. When the day shines, it is a cloudy column. When darkness comes, its mass is fire. Its presence never is withdrawn. It moves, a signal for advance. It rests, to bid them pause. Such is the safeguard of the desert-march.

Do you now ask, what is the Gospel of this sign? The type distinctly shows that no believer ever moves unled. The prophet proves this, when he selects this emblem to portray Christ's care, – 'The Lord will create upon every dwelling-place of Mount Zion, and upon her assemblies, a cloud and smoke by day, and the shining of a flaming fire by night.' Is. 4.5. The conclusion, then, is sound. The Pillar preaches Christ, the preceding Shepherd of His flock. Faith gazes on it, and drinks in the comfort of an ever-leading, never-leaving God.

Reader, come now, and seek some comfort for your pilgrim-days, from Israel's Pillar.

Especial circumstances marked it. It was but one. In mid-day brightness. and in night's deep gloom, the substance was the same. Thus Christ is ever one. He who was shadowed out in Eden, He to whom Abel looked, He who was Abraham's seed and David's offspring and the sweet theme of every prophet's harp, He who was pierced on Calvary and laid in the grave, is the same Jesus who shall shortly come again. No sinner escapes death, but through one victim, one righteousness, one faith, one hope, one clinging to one cross, one cleaving to one Lord, one journeying in one blood-stained path. There is one only Saviour of all the saved, one only door of heaven, one only plea before the judgment-seat, one only ransom of a guilty soul. If Israel had turned to other guidance, they would have rushed to sure destruction.

Reader, deluded men, with Cain-like pride, frame other saviours, and find Saviour none. Take heed. Look only to the one Christ of God, and of the Bible, and of the true church. He is not divided. Be not divided from Him.

The Pillar ever rose in firm solidity. Cloudy masses bend quickly before a driving breath. The storm beats on them, and they vanish. But this Pillar mocked the lash of hurricanes and watery floods. Amidst the roar of elements, it smiled unmoved, immovable. It was quiet, as a rock among unquiet waves.

Thus no assaults can shake salvation's column. Satan has done his worst. Each weapon which hell can point has been hurled at Him. The might and craft of man have marshalled all their forces. But every shaft of shrewdness, ridicule, and wit, the strong man's strength, the great man's greatness, the prince's power, and all plotting wiles, have fallen baffled at His feet. Reader, you may act confidence in your Guide's strength. The heavens may crumble into dust. But He cannot be shaken.

But the Pillar, in unchanging form, yet changed its aspect. In day its look was dark. In night it shone in brilliant blaze. It put on the fittest garb to gain observance. Here is the tender grace of Jesus. Mark His unwearied efforts to draw minds towards Himself. It is with this design that every Bible-page proclaims some feature of His saving truth. For this, heaven-born, heaven-taught, heaven-sent heralds in pulpits and by dying-beds, in public teaching and in private converse, call and beseech men to behold Him, as the only way of life. What more can Jesus do to cause His mercy to be fully seen? Reader, if your eyes turn elsewhere, the blame is not with the conspicuous Pillar.

When night's mantle wrapt the earth, the Pillar clad itself in robes of fire. It shone, that all might see. It shone, that all in seeing might rejoice. Such is the love of Jesus. When is His presence most clear, most cheering? Surely in the dark hour of need. When gloom oppresses, when mists of horror rise, when prospects blacken, when the beclouded eye discerns no safety and no peace in earth, then the smile of Jesus gives light. Unwonted glories then illumine the road.

The Pillar had an upraised arm. Its ascending spire directed to the skies. So Jesus calls us to an upward flight. How solemnly He warns to rise above the mire and filth of a soul-murdering world! How faithfully He tells that all its baits are poison, its touch pollution, and its wages death!

How tenderly He cries: Come unto Me, and leave such vanities below: – lean on My arm, and climb the hill of peace: – mount by My side, and I will bring you to a re-conciled Father's throne, and the high mansions of your God! Thus Jesus points. Reader, be wise. To look to Jesus is to soar to heaven.

Such were its peculiar properties. But its main pur-pose was to lead. When it preceded, the willing host ad-vanced. When it stood still, their camps were fixed. They were not called to reason, or to ask, or doubt. All wish to go or tarry submitted to the ruling column. Their guide was God. His will was love. His way was knowledge. His end was safety. Nothing was left for them, but to observe and follow.

Shall twilight types outshine the Gospel sun? It cannot be. The heirs of grace are cared for, as truly now as then. Their Leader is the same. Be it so, that Christ directs not now by visible display of manifested presence. Be it so, that the eye of nature sees not a moving or a halting mass. Still faith can trace an unseen hand, and the enlightened mind can read the warnings of a heavenly Lord.

Christ guides now by His Word. The Book of books is always by our side. It is a present and a perfect chart. The upward path, the downward slopes, the hidden snares, the plains of safety, the meadows of repose, are all here pencil-led with inspired skill. This is the blessed handbook of the blessed route. The humble pilgrim meekly prays. 'Speak, Lord, for thy servant heareth.' 1 Sam. 3.9. The answer tarries not: 'This is the way, walk ye in it.' Is. 30.21. Is it not pledged, 'When thou goest, it shall lead thee; when thou sleepest, it shall keep thee; and when thou awakest, it shall talk with thee; for the commandment is a lamp and the law is light.' Prov. 6.22, 23. The believer's daily walk attests the truth. When perils have been near, and pitfalls have gaped, and by-ways have enticed the steps, a beacon from the Word has warned and saved.

Reader, would you reach Canaan? Then cling to this ever-living guide. Search it day and night. Make it your chosen friend of every hour. Engraft it by prayer into the soul of every thought. Let it direct the helm of each desire. Think, as it thinks – speak, as it speaks – move, as it beckons – rest, as it counsels. Your steps will then be safe and pure. For the light of Scripture is the light of life. It is Christ's hand, Christ's heart. What was Israel's Pillar to our open Bible's page?

But Jesus multiplies His guiding help. He extends the superadded hand of Providence. He moves the ever-moving wheels of circumstances. No sparrow falls, no leaf decays, but in accordance with His ordering mind. He wills, and things occur. Chance is a figment of a dreaming pillow. It never was. It never can be. Thus to the child of God there is no trifle or unimportant event. Momentous issues often hang on rapid words, on sudden looks, on unintended steps. It is so, because the Lord's direction plans and overrules life's every concern. Hear Eliezer's grateful witness, 'I being in the way, the Lord led me to the house of my master's brethren.' Gen. 24.27. When Joseph's brethren thirsted for his blood, who caused the pit to hold no water? Who brought the Ishmaelites to bear him into Egypt? Who gave the sleepless night to Persia's King? Esther 6.1. Who brought the aged Simeon, the pious Anna, at the fit moment, to the temple? Luke. 2.27, 38. Who led Onesimus to hear Paul's saving words at Rome? Philem. 10.

But perhaps some mind may sometimes ask: Is this event the leading of my Lord? There are sure rules. No opening is safe which contradicts the Word. Christ's voice abroad, at home, without, within, is always one. It calls to seek God's glory, to promote redemption's kingdom, to conquer self, to tread down sloth, to flee the world's applause and lusts, to lift the standard of the cross, and to march boldly in the path of righteousness. If the path leave these lines, avoid it. Christ leads not here. Some foe misleads.

But Christ is a Pillar with more than skill to guide. There is a virtue in Him to open eyes, that they may see – to quicken feet, that they may follow – to tear reluctance from reluctant hearts. All this He effects by His almighty Spirit. Without such light, the Bible-page is a dark chaos, and wheels of Providence an intricate confusion. Sin has benumbed right sense in souls. Sin has brought blindness on the inner man. But Jesus speaks. The Spirit heals. Sight is restored. A new creation lives: and new-born powers perceive and love and tread the heavenly road.

The Pillar, too, had power to screen. It is written, 'He spread a cloud for a covering.' Ps. 105.39. The scorching rays of the sandy desert were thus warded from the journeying host.

Reader, I trust that you well know the cool retreat and sheltering covert of a Saviour's wings. The pilgrim's day is often long and hot, and darts of Satan burn with fiery sting. How soon the heart would faint, how soon the worn-out strength would fail, unless our Pillar cast a grateful shade. But it is true, 'The sun shall not smite thee by day, nor the moon by night.' Ps. 121.6.

The Pillar never failed. Provoking sins abounded. Ungrateful murmurs sent forth hateful sound. But still no wrath withdrew the guidance. It only vanished when Jordan's stream was reached.

Here is the boundless grace of Jesus. If hard iniquity could quench His love, who would not long ago have mourned His absence, and found life to be a starless night? But no! He loves, and lovingly He guides unto the end. The Pillar leaves not until the full blaze of heaven breaks forth. Like Bethlehem's star, it brings to the very place

37

where Jesus is. The beacon shines until the haven be attained. Christ leads to where Christ reigns.

Reader, whom do you follow? Think, Oh! think, whom do you follow? There are hell-ward leaders – not a few. There are downward ways, alas! – too many.

THE RED SEA

'Thus the Lord saved Israel that day out of the hand of the Egyptians.' Exod. 14.30

Israel's infancy is in a cradle of miracles. The people struggle into being amid displays of more than human help. They prosper, and prevail, in the clear sunshine of God's interposing hand. He watches over them and blesses them, not in the obscure cloak of providential arrangement, but in open manifestations of His present care.

These ancient dealings are but a map of what God's children always find. Individual experience is a clear-toned echo to this sacred page. Many a lowly heart in many a lowly hut sees, by the Spirit's light, the features of its inner life in the grand marvels of this God-led race.

Reader, come then, encamp for a few moments by the waters of the Red Sea. We may discern Christ's glories there, as plainly as on the shore of Galilee.

The host begins to march, only to find that it can march no further. The door of escape just opens to show escape receding from their grasp. The joyful morn brings in a fearful night. The budding flower hangs withered in their hand.

The moving pillar leads to destruction's jaws. The camp is pitched. And what is the station? In front break the billows of the Red Sea. Terrific barriers enclose each side. Here stands a wall of rocks, which human steps cannot surmount. There frowning forts forbid approach. But is there safety in the rear? Oh! no. The deadly foe, with deadly rage, pursues. The entangled prey is folded in despair. Surely here is the hour when hope must die. To stir is a watery grave. To stir not is to fall by cruelty's sharp scythe. The waves, the sword, alike gape ready to devour. The lashing surge, the battle-cry, speak fast-approaching death. Earth never saw poor prisoners so tightly barred.

Every child of God has some acquaintance with these straits. Through dreary years he may have slaved at bricks, beneath the yoke of hell's foul prince. At last he hears the Spirit's call to peace and freedom. He quickly strives to burst the chains. A few delighted steps are made, and Canaan's rest seems near. But suddenly fresh terrors gather round. The memory of evil days spreads as an ocean in the path. Wave upon wave presents tremendous hindrance. Behind, the thunders of the law wax loud. The fierce sword of justice glitters. On the right, nature's corruptions tower to the skies. On the left, Satan's batteries bristle with near death. These are appalling times. They only can conceive the misery, who have drunk deep draughts of spiritual distress. But let no one despair, who knows the Saviour's voice, 'Look unto Me, and be ye saved.' Is. 45.22.

Other defiles hem in the heaven-ward road. The sneers, the threats, the taunts, the false reports of persecuting men, form an impeding wall. Joseph and David, and Daniel, and other elders in the family of faith were thus encircled. But let the prayer fly upwards, 'Bring my soul out of prison that I may praise Thy name.' Ps. 142.7. And the song will soon go forth, 'He brought me forth also into a large place: He delivered me, because He delighted in me.' Ps. 18.19.

Narrow resources oft draw narrow bounds. Cherith's brook dries up. The widow says, 'I have but an handful of meal in a barrel and a little oil in a cruse.' 1 Kings 17.12 Penury obstructs the front. Increased demands cry pressingly in the rear. But broken means break not the staff of hope. He who lives on the bread of life dies not for lack of earthly grain. The pensioner on heaven's gold will always have sufficiency of this world's dross. It is not pledged in vain, 'All things are yours, – things present, and things to come.' 1 Cor. 3.21, 22.

The sequel of this history proves all this. Look now to Israel's leader. He rides above this swell of trouble, in all the calmness of unshaken faith. Firm trust in God is a bolt to keep out fear. It is a door to let in peace. The sea, the swords, the rocks, the forts, are seen by him without dismay. He knows that all is well when God precedes: – that all is safe when God protects: – that all is sure when God gives promise. He had heard, 'Certainly I will be with thee.' Exod. 3.12. The word ensures success. He had been taught that the mighty Saviour, the incarnate God, should spring from Judah's line. The tree must live which holds that seed. Towering on this rock, he commands, 'Fear ye not, stand still and see the salvation of the Lord, which He will show to you to-day.' Exod. 14.13.

'Fear ye not.' What shall they fear, above whose head the Gospel-standard floats? Faith reads thereon, 'If God be for us, who can be against us?' Rom. 8.31. But use no fruitless efforts. The waves are deep. The foes are strong. There is no help in self. 'Stand still.' Leave all to God.

Reader, here is the Gospel-warning. There is no self-salvation. No power of man can save one soul from one sin's stain. Cease, then, the vain attempt. 'Stand still.'

Here, too, are Gospel-tidings. 'See the salvation of the Lord.' Jesus alone has finished all. Alone He paid the penalty of sin. Alone He satisfied each claim of God. Alone He brought in everlasting righteousness. Alone He trod down every hindrance which guilt and hell could raise. This work is gloriously accomplished. Receive it – and you live for ever. Turn from it to self-deliverance – and self delivers you to sin's deserts.

The cheering word is added, 'The Lord shall fight for you, and ye shall hold your peace.' Exod. 14.14. Jesus is all might, all strength, all victory. All creatures which are, which have been, which shall be, are less than the least dust before Him. Who can resist when He uplifts His arm?

Believer, all this power is put forth to be your shield and sword. The wrath of man, the malice of devils, can never slay a God-defended life. The tender Shepherd cries, 'My sheep shall never perish.' John 10.28. Stand, then, behind a fighting God, and you are high as heaven above all harm. Raise not the battle-cry, as if the charge was yours. Let all your breath be prayer and praise.

And now the voice from heaven is heard. 'Speak unto the children of Israel, that they go forward.' Exod. 14.15. Here is a watchword for the Christian camp. Forward, on-ward, upward, heaven-ward, should be the daily and hourly shout.

Believer, is your life this rapidly-progressing course? Alas! how many loiter! The closing year finds them no gainers in the holy race. Others, alas, go back. They did run well. Where are they now? They paused, they lingered. Dangers threatened. Ease allured. Pleasures seduced. They turned. And can they be restored? 'O Lord God, Thou knowest.'

Believer, rally your energies. In all haste move forward, onward, upward, heaven-ward. Do overwhelming waves im-pede the way? Heed them not, if God distinctly speaks. He cannot lead you but in safety's path.

Do you say, 'Go forward' contradicts 'Stand still?' It may seem so to reason's blinded sight. But faith finds harmony, when grace gives light. We take no step to expiate our sins, to pay our debts, to appease just wrath, or to procure re-demption. While we 'Stand still,' Jesus does all. We are saved by grace, through faith. Eph. 2.8. It is the work of Jesus. It is the gift of God. But motion proves that we have life. Efforts evince that we have strength. Works evidence that we have faith. Fruit is the sign of healthy trees. Warmth is the token that gratitude's bright flame glows warmly in the heart. Heaven is reached, not by toil, but in toil. Blessings descend, not for deeds, but on deeds. Faith comes with empty hand. Christ fills it with salvation. The saved hand soon brings again the offerings of devoted love. Christ dies upon the altar of atonement. Our lives ascend, as incense to His praise. None go so surely forward to the throne as they who stand still at the saving cross.

My soul, mark next the prelude to the final scene. 'The angel of God, which went before the camp of Israel, removed and went behind them: and the pillar of the cloud went from before their face, and stood behind them. And it came between the camp of the Egyptians and the camp of Israel, and it was a cloud and darkness to them, but it gave light by night to these.' Exod. 14.19, 20.

Thus Jesus is a high wall of defence. He encompasses His blood-bought flock. They who would injure His redeemed must beat down his omnipotence. There is no passage for the destroyer's sword, but through the fort of a protecting God.

He has, however, a two-fold aspect. What floods of light flow from His smile to each believing heart! Others see nothing but the dark frown of an avenging Judge. Like the pillar, He has two sides. 'Come, ye blessed of My Father,' shines on one. 'Depart, ye cursed,' is blackly lettered on the other.

Moses now lifts his rod. This hand is first made leprous. Then it is used as a minister of miracles. God works by humbled means. He brings down. Then He exalts. Man is nothing. God is all.

The unruly billows heed the commanding sign. Submissive they retire. They open wide a passage through their trackless depths. The watery particles cement into sub-

43

stantial walls. The ransomed go forward. Impossibilities flee before them. The God of creation wills deliverance, and all creation meekly lends its help.

The children of Israel, obedient to the heavenly call, go on in faith, and reach the longed-for shore. The children of Egypt rush in presumptuously, without command. O my soul, follow God fully, and stagger not. But never move without the light of guidance from on high. Faith walks dry-shod. Presumption drowns.

For a brief moment vengeance seems to pause. But in the morning-watch the Lord looked on them, and His look was trouble. Who can conceive the power of that eye? It broke the heart of Peter. Luke 22.61, 62. It showed at once his sin and pardon. It brought the trembling woman to her knees. Luke 8.47. It made her tongue tell all. Reader, soon will it pierce each corner of your soul. 'For every eye shall see Him.' Think, will the glance of the returning Jesus seal your eternal bliss, or drive you lost into despair's abode?

The same instrument saves or destroys, as God commands. Thus the obedient waves flow back. With resistless might, they sweep the ruined to a wretched end. 'There remained not so much as one of them.' Exod. 14.28.

The Holy Spirit erects a column on the shore, and writes a worthy record. 'Thus the Lord saved Israel that day out of the hand of the Egyptians: and Israel saw the Egyptians dead upon the sea shore.' O my soul, read it in prayer, in wonder, and in praise. It tells the final glory of the Gospel: – the saved all saved:– the lost all lost.

Yes, the Lord will surely save His people with an everlasting salvation. No peril shall impede their triumph. No foe shall hinder. Trials and snares, afflictions and temptations shall make way. The grave shall not detain. Death shall yield up its prey. The true Israel shall reach the land of never-fading joy. With palms in their hands, and crowns on their heads, they shall ascribe, in ceaseless songs, all victory to the cross of Jesus.

In ruined Egypt mark the last doom of the ungodly world. Too late they see their madness. Too late they strive to flee. Reader, take warning. Perdition is a truth which many learn too late.

MARAH

'When they came to Marah, they could not drink of the waters of Marah, for they were bitter; therefore the name of it was called Marah. And the people murmured against Moses, saying, What shall we drink? And he cried unto the Lord, and the Lord shewed him a tree, which when he had cast into the waters, the waters were made sweet. Exod. 15.23, 24, 25.

Perhaps joy's bright flame was never brighter than in Israel's sons when they moved onwards from the marvels of the sea. Slavery's chain was wholly broken. Their foes lay prostrate. The Lord was for them. The Lord was with them. What more could be desired?

Can it be, that a people thus guarded, and thus guided, shall find trouble? Where the Lord precedes, can the path be other than the sunny slope of unalloyed delight? True it is, that heavenly leading is always a right way. But true it is, that the right way may be sharp with thorns, and rough with difficulties, and beset with storms. Paul's voyage was ordered, but he was sorely tossed, and hardly reached the shore.

This truth is on the forefront of Israel's truth-teaching story. 'They went three days in the wilderness, and found no water.' Exod. 15.22. Here was a sudden check to hope's high tide. They then advanced to Marah. Water there flowed. It was, however, but a mocking stream. The taste was bitter, and they could not drink.

Reader, behold two stages in the Christian chart. A grievous need occurs. A grievous disappointment presses in its rear. But let not such things move you, nor excite surprise. Are you not called to be as a richly-laden tree? Your every branch must bend with fruits of faith and hope and patience. But faith thrives most in trouble's soil. Hope's note is sweetest in the tempest's roar. Patience gains strength beneath the cross's weight. The diamond sparkles because the file is rough. Trials are needful, or they would not be. Trials are needful, therefore they abound. They walk as sisters beside goodness and mercy. They attend the believer, as appointed guards to heaven's gate. No saint sinks in these wholesome waves. But many a thoughtless soul sleeps fatally, because the downy pillow is not shaken. Learn, then, from Marah, to expect some bitter draught.

Next, Marah withdraws a veil, and we can trace the line between a graceless and a gracious heart. The host turns from God. Moses flees to Him. One looks to earth and frets. The other looks above and hopes. Believer, let me ask you, why is a throne of grace so near? Why have you open access to it? It is, that burdens may not crush you. It is, that fears may die as soon as born: that doubts may wither as a blighted bud. Mercy and grace are always strewed in rich abundance round it. Faith may take empty vessels and fill them until they overflow.

The case of Moses teaches this. He knocks. The door flies open. A ready ear hears. A ready hand supplies. The people's hard and thankless thoughts present no bar. A faithful servant cries. A loving Father grants. 'The Lord showed him a tree, which when he had cast into the waters, the waters were made sweet.'

Reader, learn next, that it is the Lord's wisdom to give relief in the use of means. He whose word called all things out of nothing could in one moment have caused salubrious springs to bubble forth. But no. A remedy is announced. Faith must trust. Obedience must comply. Diligence must work. Effort must be up and doing. The poisoned Israelites must look to the unlifted pole. The leprous Naaman must wash in Jordan seven times. The perishing sinner must flee to the crucified Jesus. The needy saint must hasten to the mercy-seat. Sloth's couch is at the gate of hell. Activities and energies scale heaven. Striving enters the strait gate. The girded loins receive the prize.

Reader, you are thus prepared to hear, that in following Jesus, your pilgrim-steps will often reach a bitter well. But murmur not. At every Marah there is a tree whose leaves drop sweetness and whose taste is balm. But bear in mind, the eye of faith alone can see it: the hand of faith alone can touch it.

Holy Spirit of the living God, we look to Thee. Increase our faith. Help us to discern, help us to apply the remedy which grace provides. Shine on this lowly effort to commend the sweetness of the 'plant of renown.' May all who read experience its healing worth!

Let us now take the cases most familiar to each pilgrim's route.

The bitterest Marah is bitterness of heart. Each heaven-bound traveller well knows this spot. The downcast Heman pitched his tent beside it. Ps. 88. The prolific fountain whence these waters spring is an accusing memory. It causes all the past to live again. At its command a train of buried sins appear in frightful freshness. They seem young as the deeds of yesterday, and hideous as the fiends of darkness. Each tells a tale which cannot be denied. Each points to fiery death as the wages of its work. Each shows an open prison-door. Each shakes the chain of ruin's cell. Well may the stricken conscience quake. A stern voice, too, is heard, Can he who sinned these sins have hope of life? Hell's jailer sneers, You will be mine at last. Who can drink this wormwood and survive?

But sweet relief is near. Jesus, the tree of life, extends His bending branches to the anxious touch. Let the poor sinner boldly shake it. A shower of healing leaves falls thick. Each yields the honey of these honeyed tidings, 'I, even, I, am He, that blotteth out thy transgressions for mine own sake, and will not remember thy sins.' Is. 43.25. 'As far as

the east is from the west, so far hath He removed our transgressions from us.' Ps. 103.12. When such relief is inter-
mixed, the hateful taste gives place. The virtue of a Saviour's death extracts all poison from the cup.

Another Marah soon appears. The believer is tempted to
seek refreshment from some inward source. Then nothing
meets him but a brackish pool. What is man's heart, but
the loathsome depths of the Dead Sea? Adam's first sin
defiled the fountain-head, and poisoned springs give nought
but poisoned streams. Alas! what ceaseless currents of corruptions force their way! Who has not cause to mourn with
Paul, 'When I would do good, evil is present with me'?
Rom. 7.21. What raging passions, what unruly tempers,
what vile desires, what godless thoughts, what vain con-
ceits, pollute our cisterns with their noxious fluid! The best
of nature is a miry ditch. Is there no help? There is, in the
all-sweetening tree. Jesus presents His cure. Welcome the
hallowing Saviour, and grace will distil from Him, to make
each stagnant marsh a rivulet of health. He can create a new
heart, and renew a right spirit. He can sanctify wholly. He
can preserve pure and blameless. He can work in us both to
will and to do of His good pleasure. No Marah is so bitter
as the heart when Christ is absent. No spring is so health-
giving as the heart which Christ inhabits.

There is another Marah in the world's keen hate. Enmity
still separates the seed of the serpent and the seed of Christ.
The race of Ishmael still persecutes the child of promise.
Gal. 4.29. Motives are mistaken. Words are distorted. Love
for souls is reviled as affectation of superior light. To warn
of danger seems to boast of self. Zeal for truth is termed
a party-strife. To depart from evil is pharisaic pride. This
draught is bitter to a tender spirit. But Christ can make it
sweet. His arms of love especially embrace His suffering
witnesses. The music of His whispers drowns the harsh

thunder of the hardest threats. Daniel will tell you that his sweetest night was in the lion's den. The captive children never felt heaven nearer than in the chamber of the flames. Paul never sang more joyously than in the inner cell. View, too, the glorious martyrs of our blessed church. They clasped the stake. They revelled in the fires. Jesus was with them. They drank of the bitterest brook. But there was no bitterness therein.

Believer, perhaps you go heavily because of some personal or domestic smart. Few are unused to this affliction's gloom. Is it your case, that nights are pain, and the returning light brings langour? Does your frame totter as a reed? Is sickness your consuming guest? This is your Marah. Bitter indeed it is to nature's palate. But I am bold to uplift Jesus, as ready to make even this well all sweet. Failing strength is not a sign of failing interest in a Saviour's heart. Lazarus was loved. Yet Lazarus was sick. John 11.1. Feeble may be the cry. But feeble cries are strong to move our sympathising Head. His precious cordials will revive the drooping spirit. Can He be present, and joy not sit beside Him? How many languid smiles attest that hours of pain are earnests of the painless heaven!

Perhaps poverty may touch your store with withering hand? You once were full; you now are empty. This is your Marah. Who will deny that the trial is most grievous? But experience in God's Word and ways will prove, that this cup may run over in abundance of content. There is no empty coffer to him who sings, 'The Lord is my Shepherd, I shall not want.' Ps. 23.1. Elijah had no bursting barns. But heaven-sent messengers supplied his earliest and his latest needs. The faith which finds all things in Christ extracts all gall from penury.

Do you sit in bereavement's solitude? Is a much-loved form no longer seen? Is a much-loved voice no longer heard? This is your Marah. The cup is bitter. But Jesu's comforts blossom most when earthly flowers die. He lives, and lives to heal your weeping wounds. Ask the mourning widow of Nain who changed her sorrow into joy. Luke 7.14. Ask the disconsolate sisters of Bethany who dried their tears. The quick reply is – Jesus. Has He ceased to pity? Can His tenderness grow hard? It cannot be. His presence can fill, and more than fill each void.

Reader, there is another Marah. The brink of it is at your feet. Another step may reach the stream of death. The waters here seem often to be very bitter. But Jesus has efficacy to make them sweet. Approach, then, leaning on His arm, trusting in His cross, hidden in His wounds, covered by His righteousness, and you will find the taste to be all joy. The bitterness of death is sin unpardoned. But the blood which takes away all sin, takes out all poison.

When you have passed this brook, all Marahs are behind you. But what is the flood which now stretches onward and onward, without limit, without shore? It is the heaven of God's pleasures. It is the ocean of God's glory. The redeemed drink for ever. And as they drink, the depth seems deeper, and the sweetness sweeter.

Reader, are you a stranger to a Saviour's grace? If so, your dwelling now is always at a Marah's side. Your daily well holds the bitter water of vanity, vexation, sorrow, disappointment, discontent. Time bears you swiftly to the final stage. What then? There is the cup of trembling and of wrath. Your hands must take it. Your mouth must drink. But you can never drain it. There is no last drop. Infinite vengeance ever fills it to the brim. Eternal wrath is ever bringing more. The merciless tormentor, with unwearied savageness, presents it to the lips.

Reader, think of the rich man and his uncooled tongue. Luke 16.24. Think of the redeemed. 'The Lamb, which is in the midst of the throne shall feed them, and shall lead them unto living fountains of waters.' Rev. 7.17.

THE HEALER

'I am the Lord that healeth thee.' Exod. 15.26

These words first cheered the heart of Moses. But they are the common heritage of the Church of God. This day they reach our ears. May they bring healing on their wings!

Reader, in thought survey the porches of Bethesda's pool. (John 5.). Can earth present a sight of deeper woe? Malady makes every form its prey. Each sound is burdened with a sufferer's groan. The heart is hard which can repress the sigh, Oh! that these pains might end! But vain may be the wish. For human ailment often baffles human skill. It knows no certain cure.

Are you prepared to see your own case in those cells? Transfer the sickness from the body to the soul, and then your couch is surely spread among these sufferers. Sin makes this world a world-large hospital. It drives earth's millions into one Bethesda.

Reader, do you sigh here, Oh! that these deeper pains might end! This speedily may be. There is one sure relief. Jesus stands near, a spiritual Healer, mighty to cause the blind to see, the deaf to hear, the lame to walk, the leprous to be clean, and every wound to close. No case exceeds His healing power.

These lines are written, that sin-diseased souls may now be led to drink at this truth's fount.

Holy Spirit! grant Thine aid. Show that the malady of sin abounds throughout man's tribes. Show that all remedy much more abounds in Christ.

The cure will be more prized, if first we mark the many features of our deep disease. Let us remove the mask, then, and behold the multiform malignity of this fiend – sin.

Sin is a universal taint. No child of man escapes it. We tread this earth diverse in clime, in station, in mental power, in mould of temper, and in frame of limb. But all who breathe life's breath are spotted with this plague. Adam's foul fall infused the evil poison into nature's veins. Each parent sows this seed. No progeny is infection-free. Cain was conceived in sin. The latest babe must be corruption's heir.

Reader, your cradle may have been wealth's down, or poverty's hard board. You may have intellect to command a wondering world's applause, or you may crawl unknown to an unknown grave. In these externals no two may be one. But all are one in oneness of distempered soul. Each mother's infant is transgression's child.

Sin is an all-spoiling evil. It is a weed which over-runs the garden. It stains all men, and every part in each. It enters to pervade. Its root is in the soul. Eden saw it planted there. But its fibres and its branches spread through each faculty of mind and body. See how it masters the whole inner frame. The heart first sickens. This becomes harder than the nether millstone, the nest of every unclean bird, the den of lust's vile brood. The head soon grows distempered. Hence error and ignorance expel right judgment. The world is worshipped as a rightful lord. Hell is derided as some weak fable. Repentance is reserved for dying moments. The glorious word is scorned as the bewildered page in which the brain-sick and fanatic glean delusions. The eye is blind to see the 'chief among ten thousand, the altogether lovely.' The ear hears nought but discord in the Gospel-note. The palate has no relish of salubrious food. The lips, the mouth, the throat, the tongue, are festered with contaminating sores. Alas! how many words go forth to spread contagion and to scatter death. Thus the disease runs wildly through the whole man.

Sin is the union of all spiritual maladies in one com-pacted mass. It is no single evil. It comes in troops, in flocks, in swarms. In our frames one member may be weak, the others strong. But in this hospital, all sufferings at once make every sufferer their prey. One ailment is all ailments. One part infected leaves no part in health.

Sin never yields to earth-born cure. All trials have been tried. But failure is the end of each. Self has ransacked the stores of self. Wounds have been washed with tears, and bound with bands of stricter life. The cup of penance and of rigid vow has oft been drunk with eager lip. But remedy is not in these. A feather stays not the fast-rushing stream. A little pruning kills not the branch. Oil will not quench a flame.

Shall then the sin-sick fly to forms and ceremonies and hallowed rites? Alas! their anguish lies too deep for super-ficial cure. Uplifted hands and bended knees, and all the sacredness of sacred things, have in themselves no virtue to choke evil's fount. The love of holy service is a sign of health. But it cannot confer it. Restored cripples leap and walk and praise as evidence of strength, but not to gain it. No human medicines give soul-health.

Sin's end is endless death. Its course is sure. The falling stone rolls downward to the lowest depths. The stream flows on until the ocean's bed is reached. Thus sin's strong bias rushes to the pit of hell. Oh! mark those writhing sufferers in the burning lake. Ask them what brought them to their woe. One wild shriek answers, Sin – Sin uncured, unchecked. Ah! sinner, your inward malady seems little now. What will it prove, hereafter? Its present touch gives little smart, but it has iron arms. The embrace seems gentle now. But it will tighten into ever-tightening torture.

This sketch is dark. The reality is darker far. But why are these black colours laid? The purport is, to form a background for the Scripture-light. The malady's malignity is drawn to show that one Physician only can avail.

Look now toward the chambers of the Gospel-east. The horizon gleams with rays. The Sun of Righteousness appears; and there is 'healing in his wings.' Amid Bethesda's crowded seats, the blessed Jesus stood, omnipotent to heal. Amid the soul-sick, He as surely stands with like omnipotence. He comes, and His voice is, 'I am the Lord that healeth thee.' Behold His outstretched hands. They bear a perfect remedy. He takes away sin's poison, and it cannot kill. He soothes its wounds, and they can no more pain. He cuts its roots, and they can no more spread.

Come, hear these tidings from His Word of Truth.

Your first complaint is, that your sickness is the seed of everlasting death. True! It is dragging you with rapid force towards a gaping grave. But Jesus takes your sins and nails them to His cross. Then in His death they die. Then in His wounds they disappear. He washes you with His heart's blood. He bathes you in this precious stream. And never, never are your sins found again. Thus condemnation is for ever gone. Is not that sickness healed which has no power to harm? Thus Jesus is the sinner's Healer. He brings in pardon. Pardon changes malady to health, because it changes death to life. Believer, you are thus relieved. Let your song ever be, He forgiveth all mine iniquities – and so He heals all my diseases. Ps. 103.3.

But you still sigh that, though future punishment is gone, yet present pain still gnaws. The scar may smart which is not unto death. You are a guilt-touched wretch. And sense of guilt is an unceasing ache. Truly these tears are bitter. But in Jesus there is solace for these pangs. No ease can come, but by the Spirit's hand. He only takes it from the Saviour's blood. But He brings soothing virtue thence and lulls the accusing conscience into rest. He can present, as an assuaging cup, the tender promise, 'I will forgive their iniquity, and I will remember their sin no more.' Jer. 31.34. He can apply the calming argument: Wherefore should memory dwell sobbingly on what God casts behind His back for ever? He can teach, that a head crowned with pardon's crown should not hang down. Thus Jesus fulfils the word; He gives 'unto them beauty for ashes, the oil of joy for mourning.' Is. 61.3.

Thus sin is cured because its pain is soothed. Believer, will you not confess. He 'is sent to heal the broken-hearted'?

But you may add, that more is needed to restore full health. You mourn that the vile roots lie deep within. No child of God is unconscious of the lurking evil. While the flesh is flesh, it is the hot-bed of corruption. But Jesus can subdue the plague. By sanctifying grace He can create a clean heart and renew a right spirit. He can implant a counteracting principle of godly love. He can give strength to fight the good fight of faith, to run with patience in pure paths, and to find no delight but in God's will. O my soul, cling then to the cross. In its atmosphere evil withers, and saintliness grows firm.

Thus Jesus cures all sin. It can no more condemn nor vex nor rule. They walk in healthy peace with God, in healthy peace within, in healthy paths of holy life, whose hearts have heard, 'I am the Lord that healeth thee.'

Perhaps you still fear, lest the extreme malignity of your case should baffle all this skill. It would be so, except the Healer were Jehovah-Jesus. But mark. His title shivers all such doubts. He cries 'I am the Lord that healeth thee.' Almightiness is the property of this arm. He wills, and it is done. He works, and none can thwart. If all the maladies of all the sufferers in earth and hell formed one huge sickness centring on your soul, let Christ the Lord but speak, and perfect is your cure.

Are you disquieted, lest long lying on sin's couch should bar against you every door of hope? Consider well the Healer. At Bethesda's pool he singles out the wretchedness of him who 'had been now a long time in that case.' Extremity of misery was a melting plea. His heart is still the same. Take courage. If, from the day of Adam's fall, your malady had rolled onward as a swelling stream, His tender love could turn it all to health.

Does conscience groan beneath the load of signal provocations? You may have turned from many a gracious call. This very case is met by mercy's sweet voice. Read your sure welcome in the page of life. 'He went on frowardly in the way of his heart. I have seen his ways, and will heal him.' Is. 57.17, 18.

You reply, that the hand of faith alone can take the remedy. But your faith so trembles that it scarcely lives. Behold the timid woman of the Gospel. With down-cast eye, with tottering step, she comes, and instantly the touch was life. Do but the same: and you will hear, 'Thy faith hath made thee whole; go in peace.' Mark 5.34.

Shall all this earnest pleading fail? It only remains, then, to pray again that the all-conquering Spirit would make you willing to be among the Healer's healed ones. Oh! look to Jesu's cross. It was ordained of old. It was erected on Calvary. It is uplifted in the Gospel. It is magnified in every faithful pulpit. But why? Surely that miseries may end, and spiritual diseases may be cured. On it the Heavenly Healer dies Himself, that His death may be the death of sin. On it He bleeds, that His blood may drop soundness. On it He suffers wounds, that the wounded may be whole. On it He gives His body to most painful pains, that ease may be His people's portion. On it He lays down His life, that they may have life. And now He cries, Come, without money, without price. Come, leave your sickness, and return with health.

MANNA

'It is Manna.' Exod. 16.15

Food was provided for the chosen tribes, unseen before by human eye, untouched before by human hand. 'They wist not what it was.' Exod. 16.15.

Reader, when here the Manna is presented to your view, I hope it comes as a familiar thought. It is faith's wont to lay it up in memory's ark, as the rich emblem of Salvation's feast.

Manna has many tongues. But its first sound proclaims, that God is gracious. Mark the occasion of these showers of bread. Hunger pressed sore upon the journeying host, and pressed vile murmurs from their fretful hearts. The deep-toned mutters reached the courts on high. Will the swift lightning check rebellious madness? Oh! no. The Lord is pitiful, and delights in love. He opens heaven to pour down supplies. The supply is a miracle. The miracle is a wreath of combined wonders. Each wonder is a rich display of Jesus, and teaches now, as clearly as it fed of old. Thus God puts on a diadem of grace, and crowns the thankless with most tender mercies.

But goodness in bestowing food is taper-grace beside the shinings of redemption's gift. They who would see grace in its zenith must trace it in the Gospel-scheme. When the whole family of man, in Adam's loins, stood before God, lost, ruined, and undone – one leprous mass of misery and sin – shameless, tearless, prayerless – mercy took up the song, and promised that a Saviour should descend, even an incarnate God. Reader, your heart is rock indeed, if you hear this, and give no praises to Jehovah's grace.

It was all dark around, when this soft shower reached our

earth. We read, 'When the dew fell upon the camp in the night, the Manna fell upon it.' Num. 11.9. So spiritual blindness was the world's thick shroud when Jesus came, distilling blessing from His wings. So when His gentle droppings first touch the sinner's heart, He finds it a black mass of midnight gloom.

When morning came, the dew dissolved and left the Manna obvious to the sight. Thus for a while Jesus lies hid in the word, and ordinances, and Gospel-rites, which fall in thick and sparkling abundance around our homes. It is not until the Sun of Righteousness arise, that the real treasure is discerned. Then unsubstantial privileges fade off, and Christ remains the whole of soul-support. Reader, the dew was a fit mantle for this heaven-sent food. But it has neither taste nor vital juice. Just so the means of grace are lovely caskets of the heavenly treasure. But he who would have life must pass beyond them to the Lord Himself.

The Manna was small, and round, and white, and sweet. Each property tells much of Jesu's worth into the ear of faith.

It was small. It lay a little seed upon the bare earth. Pride would take up a ready sneer. Can this mean mite proceed from heaven's store?

Jesus appears. No royal state surrounds. No royal home receives. No royal retinue attends. In lowly guise, He seems the lowliest of lowly men. His highest station upon earth is in humility's deep vale. But meekness is His Majesty. Abasement is His Glory. Believer, He puts on your flesh, that He may clothe you in His brightest glory. He sinks to nothingness, to exalt you above all greatness. He lives and dies in shame, contempt, and pain, that you may reign in all the honours of the highest heavens. Your blessings bud forth from His mean estate.

The Manna was round. The hand which handled found no first and no last point. It was a surface without beginning, without end. Behold the wondrous Jesus. Who can ascend to the springhead of His birth? Who can stretch forward to the boundary of His life? Who can discern a limit in the circles upon circles of His being? Look through the ages of eternity past. In all He lives unchanged, unchangeable. Look through the ages of eternity to come. He still lives unchanged, unchangeable. Believer, is not this thought an ocean of delight, wide as the breadth and length of your Saviour's love? He never was, but with your image on His heart. And while He lives, your image will be there.

The Manna was white. It covered the mire of earth, a bright contrast to surrounding stains. Its spotless hue proved its descent to be from a pure home. Turn now to Jesus. His every look and word and step are dazzling, as the holiness of heaven. He was the Righteousness of God embodied in the flesh of man. He trod this earth, perfect as God is perfect. He ever shone untainted, as the beam from the mid-day sun. It could not be otherwise. Deity forbad. Impossibility of sin is Jehovah's essence. It must be so. Redemption needed it. He who would save a soul from sin must give the offering of a sinless soul. Reader, would you be blameless before God? Put on Christ Jesus.

The Manna was sweet. The palate tasted, and delighted in the luscious savour. It nourished, and the nourishment brought pleasure to the lips. This is the Saviour's emblem. He is all sweetness to the feasting soul. Is it not heaven's own luxury to feed upon divine assurances that all sins are fully and for ever pardoned:– all guilt fully and for ever cancelled:– all debts fully and for ever paid:– all pledges of glory faithfully and for ever pledged? Is it not sweet to gaze with open eye on a reconciled Father's smile:– to receive unmeasured comfort, instruction, strength, and guidance from the indwelling Spirit:– to realise, that ministering angels encamp around:– that good men love us, evil men serve us, and all things present and to come are our sure heritage? Jesus is this sweet Manna. Is it not sweet to be regaled all day at such a banquet, to repose all night on such a pillow, to walk through life in such green pastures? This is the believer's Manna. Worldling, is your repast thus sweet?

Each day the host was busy in the field. The constant food fell thick, the constant hand collected. O my soul, let gathering be your daily work. Time is prolonged, that you may thrive. And what is thriving, but to gain more truth? The worldling toils a live-long toil in gleaning husks. Can you sit still, when Christ is to be won? Believe me, that is your richest day which hives the most of Him. Your best, without Him, is an empty blank.

They went forth early. The sun's first beams lighted them to their happy task. Here mark, how morning diligence succeeds. It is the truest wisdom, the surest peace, the largest profit, when opening day finds you with open heart before the mercy-seat, with open lip adoring God, with open Bible seeking the Lord. The arrow long retains the first direction of the impelling hand. The vessel rarely loses the savour of its first contents. The day-break blessing is a day-long gain. Let Jesus draw back your morning-curtain, and He will sanctify the mid-day labour, and lull you to the night's repose.

Perhaps some youthful eye is resting on this page. Beloved, turn not from a wise entreaty. Give to the Lord the first fruits of your being. He is worthy, for He is all worthiness. He calls you with especial grace. 'Those that seek me early, shall find me.' Prov. 8.17. And finding Him, you find an ever-blessing portion. Apart from Him, you must be lost. In Him you shall be saved. All is a wilderness of woe without Him. All is a Paradise of joy beside Him. If angels sing with sweeter song, methinks it must be round a Christian youth. Come then betimes. Come now. None ever came too soon. Many, alas, have sought too late!

For every hand there was exact sufficiency. 'He, that gathered much, had nothing over; and He that gathered little had no lack.' Exod. 16.18. Infinite are each poor sinner's sins; and each has infinite demerit. Boundless is the unrighteousness of every soul, boundless the covering which is needed. Countless are the wants which cry for countless helps. But he who lives bathing in a Saviour's blood, and suing out a Saviour's righteousness, and wrestling for a Saviour's grace, will never say that the blood, the righteousness, the grace, exceed his daily need. He gets enough, but he has nought to spare. He, too, who flees at last, and only touches with a trembling hand the extremest edge of Jesu's robe, if it be but the touch of heaven-born faith, receives full pardon and eternal life. A crumb of Jesu's merits is the saving of the soul for ever.

The daily food was only for the day. To hoard was to distrust the daily-giving hand. A mass became corruption, to be buried out of sight.

So, too, in grace, the present handful is for present use. The morrow's dearth will have the morrow's shower. Away with chilly fears. The Manna came as surely as the light. Jesus never fails to pour His plenties down. Trade, then, with the present stock. The worst of cases is the case of grace misused. The buried talent cries with condemning voice. Christ not diffused is Christ misused. Treasure is not enjoyed till it be well employed. He is most rich, who most enriches others.

For every state and age the Manna was but one. One is the dreadful plague. One is the precious cure. The highest palace and the humblest cot, the lettered hall and the unlettered cabin, the aged bed, the cradle of the young, alike are tainted with one leprous spot. One only remedy meets the one malady – the remedy of the life and death of Christ.

The Manna came not through man's toil. But still it came not to encourage sloth. Active art must grind and sweeten for the use. Vain is it that Christ with all salvation is at the door, vain is the Bible-store, vain is the pulpit-food, except the eager soul gird up the loins of eager doing. Faith labours all the day to draw out sweetness from the Gospel-page. With skilful care it sifts each word. With anxious appetite it sucks the sweet.

The Manna preaches, too, with wisdom's voice. It cries, Keep holy the Sabbath-day. It comes from heaven, therefore it proclaims God's law. It comes to be a blessing, therefore it points to obedience as the path. When will man's blindness learn that there is no profit, and no peace, but in the ways and will of God? Who ever gained in Sabbath-shops, or by a Sabbath-spade? From the seed of Sabbath-work springs up a harvest of soul-piercing woe. Israel's rest was never Israel's loss.

The Manna sustained the body for a little while. But it was weak to blunt the shafts of death. In the wilderness they ate and died. But Christ gives endless life to each partaking soul. Reader, drink in the tidings, 'I am the living bread, which came down from heaven: if any man eat of this bread, he shall live for ever: and the bread that I will give is My flesh, which I will give for the life of the world.' John 6.51.

Lord, increase my faith! Help me to see in Thy body broken, all that I need for strength, for vigour, and for joy of heart. The more we crave, the more we get. The more we get, the more we crave.

The Manna lasted through the desert-march. Thus Jesus is supply for all life's weary way. And when time's crumbs are no more needed, eternity's full feast begins. Sweet is the present taste of grace: but what will be the heavenly board?

My soul, press onward – and you soon will know.

THE SMITTEN ROCK

'Thou shalt smite the rock, and there shall come water out of it, that the people may drink.' Exod. 17.6

It was a bitter trial when Marah's bitter spring mocked the parched lip. But sweet relief was near. The sweetened draught soon changed vexation into joy. After a little pause the same dark trial re-appears in darker form. The multitude advance into the desert's depths. And here all streams quite fail. They thirst and search, but search in vain. The scene is universal drought. Thus troubles die and live again.

This is a common circumstance in faith's march. Afflictions clear away; but soon the self-same shades grow thick. Joseph escapes the pit, and then the dungeon binds him fast. David, safe from Adullam's cave, must seek a refuge in Engedi's wilds. Troops, too, of lusts which seemed through grace, quite slain in former days, with mustered force will re-assail old age. The weeds of evil, long plucked up, will rear again their noxious head. Satan lays Abraham low in Egypt, and shoots an arrow from the same shaft in Gerar. Gen. 12.18, 20.2. The falling spoke of the revolving wheel soon re-ascends. The ebbing tide rolls in again to-morrow.

Believer, think not of undisturbed repose until the flesh be dropped. There is a ceaseless cycle of sorrow and temptation here. But despise not the scourge. It has a teaching voice. It is held by a loving Father's hand. Hence the command, 'Hear ye the rod, and who hath appointed it.' Mic. 6.9. This school of trial best discloses the hidden vileness of the heart, and the vast riches of a Saviour's grace.

It is so in the case before us. The hard repinings of the chosen race betray poor nature's bias. But on rebellion's base a lovely pillar rises, on which all ages read the golden glories of the Lord.

The people chide, and tempt their God. Moses seeks the open refuge of a mercy-seat. How precious is this spot! A gracious answer soon allays all fears, and soon supplies all need. The Lord said, 'Go on before the people and take with thee of the elders of Israel; and thy rod, wherewith thou smotest the river, take in thine hand, and go. Behold, I will stand before thee there upon the rock in Horeb: and thou shalt smite the rock, and there shall come water out of it, that the people may drink.' Exod. 17.5, 6.

Reader, draw near in reverence. The ground is holy. That Rock is Christ. That fissure is His wounded side. Those streams are His abundant grace.

First sift the foremost thoughts which the idea of rock presents. It is a mass of mighty strength. The lashing billows lash in vain. The raging storm stirs not its fixed repose. All changing ages find it still unchanged.

These properties exhibit Christ. Mark His decrees. Eternal love arranged salvation's scheme. The hand of sovereign grace drew the wise record of His wondrous kingdom. This chart is framed for ever. To blinded reason chance may seem to rule, and man's wild will to hold the helm. But all things serve the counsels of His plan. The falling sparrow and the tottering throne, the fading leaf, and the declining empire, obey a fixed resolve. His purpose cannot be moved. He is a Rock.

Survey His wondrous love. It yearns over a vast multitude of ruined souls. It calls them to His knowledge. It gives them pledges of His zeal to save. How is this love requited? Alas! what cold indifference, what hard ingratitude, what proud contempt, what daring rebellion, what ceaseless provocations, concur to shut up His loving-kindness in displeasure! But still, He loves unto the end of endless ages. And why? He is a Rock.

When He sought earth on mercy's wings, all powers of evil met Him with their deadliest force. The might of Satan is the united might of fallen spirits. With what ease he sweeps his crowds from earth to hell! With what resistless power he forges chains to bind men in the fiery lake! He put forth all his efforts to lay Jesus low. But every aim recoiled. The battering blows were death-blows to himself. Jesus stands as a Rock.

Reader, this Rock is near, your one support, your only refuge. Be wise, and lay your every sin on Him. The weight indeed would weigh down worlds. But He can bear all. He can bear all away. Be wise, and cast your every care on Him. Cares come indeed with rapid tide, and threaten to overwhelm. But let them waft you to the mercy-seat, where Jesus waits to take them. In faith and prayer roll them on Him. They cannot over-burden Him. He is a Rock.

Moses must smite the Rock. And do not blows fall heavily on Christ? He comes to undergo all penalties of sin. The holy Law has spoken from its holy throne. In all the majesty of God it has denounced unutterable and immeasurable woe on every breach of its most glorious code. Transgression is an inevitable curse. The statutes of heaven would be a trifler's jest, the threats of God would be an unmeaning tale, unless this vengeance in its utmost fury fall. Who can pass heaven's gate by trampling on heaven's edicts? The Word, severe in righteousness and righteous in severity, must reign inviolate. The stricken Jesus is proof that it is so. The Surety-God meets the violated law. Can it spare Him? To spare Him is to make salvation void. It spares Him not. The command is, Smite the Rock. The antitype is the smitten Jesus. He gives His back to the relentless vengeance, until by His stripes His people are all freed. He is smitten for them. They are smitten in Him. He dies for them. They die in Him. The Rock receives fast-falling blows. Thus it is shelter, and the sheltered are unharmed.

These sufferings of the bleeding Lamb are the brightness and the glory of our Bible. Let the cross vanish, let the agony be put aside, let the dying cry be no more heard, and what is the Gospel message? Its promises deceive. Its hope is wild despair. Its peace is torture. Its life is endless death. Its freedom rivets stronger chains. They who trust in it lean on a piercing reed. They who plead it plead a betraying plea. It is an atonement which atones not. It is expiation which removes no guilt. It is satisfaction which answers no demand. It is redemption which pays no price. It is salvation which saves no soul. But blessed be the gracious God of all grace! the cross erects its heaven-high head throughout the Scriptures. A bruised God-man bleeds thereon. In his heart the sword of Justice is hidden to its very hilt. Jehovah's fellow exhausts Jehovah's wrath.

Reader, mark well the smitten Rock. Behold these clefts. They gape to screen offenders from pursuing rage. Flee to them. Enter in. Hide yourself, your soul, your sins, in those deep wounds. Secreted there, you are safe, safe from all foes, safe for all ages. No curse can touch you. No wrath can find you. Satan cannot reach you. Guilt cannot ruin you. The pierced side is God-wrought, God-strong refuge.

But to return to Horeb's riven side. The host needs water. But can the hard stone melt into running streams? Yes! All things can change their nature at their Maker's will. To serve His people the sea congeals, the flint dissolves. Believer, this is a marvel which your own heart knows. It once was as the nether-millstone. But struck by the Spirit's rod, it flows a rivulet of faith, and gratitude, and praise, and love. When Jesus is uplifted, scorn may demand, Can blessings break forth from that pierced side? Yes! By those stripes the heaven of heavens opens, all hindrances remove, and a wide channel spreads for grace upon grace to flow. The wounds of Jesus are the Spirit's avenue. They send forth blood indeed to purchase pardon. They give forth water, too, the sparkling emblem of the power of grace.

Sweet was this blessing to the pilgrims of the desert. It allayed all thirst, it cleansed all stains, it cooled when heat oppressed. But sweeter far are spiritual supplies from the true Rock to the true sons of God. Gracious souls are as the gaping soil. They thirst, they daily thirst for clearer views of God, for deeper knowledge of redeeming love, for brighter light on Gospel-hopes. And they thirst not in vain. The Spirit gives deep cups of glorious truth. They drink with gladness, and their hearts rejoice. He is most happy who lives the nearest to this stream.

Gracious souls need constant cleansing. They mourn corruptions which still live within them. With hateful wing their thoughts and feelings hover over evil's mire. They pant for inward purity. For this the Spirit's help is near. He sprinkles clean water on their wills and ways, and thus preserves them from the hated filth. He is most holy who draws most water from this fount.

Gracious souls are often pierced with fiery darts. The flames of passion irritate and scorch. Nothing in self, nothing of earth can give the cooling ease. They long, with David, 'Oh! that one would give me drink of the water of the well of Bethlehem.' 2 Sam. 23.15. The Spirit hears, and calming promises are soon applied. He is most peaceful whom sheltering wings protect and soothing streams refresh.

Through the long way, Horeb's supply was ever near. When Israel stirred and stayed, the water babbled by their side. So neither place nor time nor state can check the mighty Spirit's flow. All praying lips shall always quaff, 'If ye, then, being evil, know how to give good gifts unto your children, how much more shall your heavenly Father give the Holy Spirit to them that ask Him.' Luke 11.13.

The gift was free. The wealthy and the poor alike required and alike received. So, too, the call of grace is wide as earth and long as time. 'Whosoever will, let him take of the water of life freely.' Rev. 22.17. Do any fear lest the pure stream may flee the touch of unclean lips? The type forbids the doubt. The hardest murmurer in the camp partook. The Spirit scorns not a poor sinner's heart.

Reader, would you be blessed, and a blessing? Drink oft, drink more of this inspiring stream. The grace-receiving are the grace-diffusing. They who live near to heaven attract to heaven.

At Kadesh, Miriam's praising lips were closed in death. And then the flowing boon seemed checked. Num. 20.2. What shall be done? The heavenly Teacher wisely teaches, 'Speak unto the rock, and it shall give forth its waters.' Num. 20.8. It is for ever true, 'Ask, and ye shall have.'

Moses in haste again uplifts the rod. Where was his faith? Was his eye dim to the full light of this clear Gospel type? The rock was smitten once for all. No further stroke was needed or allowed. Christ suffers once. His one grand sacrifice is sin's one death. The wound once given buys remission of all guilt for ever. Believe, delight, and glory in the one cross. It is enough. It is an all-sufficient price. The thought of repetition is ignorance, distrust, and blasphemy. O blessed Jesus! Thy one offering is all salvation. I would pray unto Thee with every breath, but woe unto me, if I bid Thee die again.

Worldling, you rest not on this Rock, but on the sand. Your hope fast crumbles. Flee from it, ere it sink into perdition. You drink not of these healthful waters, but of a poisoned puddle. The present taste is bitter – you thirst again, and thirst in vain. Beware, lest soon, in hopeless thirst, you wail for one drop to cool a tongue tormented in the flame.

PREVAILING INTERCESSION

'It came to pass, when Moses held up his hand,
that Israel prevailed: and when he let down his hand,
Amalek prevailed.' Exod. 17.11

Alarms soon trouble the advancing host. Amalek attacks their rear. Esau's tribe has evil will against the house of Jacob. The birthright sold, the blessing lost, had deeply laid the seeds of malice. And now occasion ripens hatred into fierce assault.

Believer, the race of Cain, of Ishmael, of Esau still lives. Be ready. Their hate is sure. Their wily steps are near. When least expected, they will plot their worst.

How shall such foes be met? He who follows Christ must neither fly nor yield nor fear. He must stand fast in faith, and he must kneel in prayer. So Moses teaches. He commands Joshua, 'Choose us out men, and go out, fight.' Exod. 17.9. Heaven's crown sits only on a warrior's brow.

But carnal weapons are impotent alone. In fighting, not by fighting, we prevail. So when Joshua struggles in the plain, Moses wrestles on the hill. He seeks the summit, bearing the rod. Prayer brings all heaven to the aid. Thus Israel's hands are strong or weak as those of Moses rise or drop.

Large Gospel lessons here expand before us. We may roam up and down this field and find no end in gathering precious fruit. But one especial tree calls us to shake its richly-laden boughs.

Moses interceding on the hill shows Jesus interceding on the higher heights.

Come then, my soul, with joyful wing fly upward. It is good, it is wise, it is blessed, to be much with Jesus in the suffering vale. Faith visits oft the manger, the garden, and the cross. It seeks all sin's remission in the stripes, the wounds, the agony, the death of the bleeding Lamb. But these amazing truths are but the porch of more amazing glories. Hence it delights to follow Jesus in His bright ascent, to gaze undazzled on the throne, to mark His present doings by His Father's side.

What? Is He still engaged in work? Wondrous tidings! Hear, all who call Him Lord: He ever loves you, and ever labours in your cause. His eye is never turned away. His hands cannot hang down. His heavens are the office-chamber of your soul's concerns.

Do you ask, What is His work? Hark, the Holy Spirit cries, 'He ever liveth to make Intercession.' Heb. 7.25. His every day and every hour is ceaseless energy of interceding love.

Do you add, But what is Intercession? An intercessor stands between two parties, praying the one to look with favour on the other. The persons here are God the Father, and poor worms of earth. 'If any man sin, we have an Advocate with the Father, Jesus Christ the righteous.' 1 John 2.1, 2.

Before the Father, then, the Mediator pleads. But is not the Father an overflowing ocean of free grace? Is it not His grand delight to crown His sons with all heaven's blessings? Why, then, shall prayers, like constant incense, move Him to give what He is unwilling to withhold? Salvation's scheme is wholly ordered to show forth love in brightest rays. It is to aid this end, that Intercession has its place.

Believer, what kindles flames of comfort in your heart? What decks your brow with smiles, when trials and temptations throng? Is it not a view of Jesus pleading at God's right hand? The thought is rapture, peace, and victory. Remove the Advocate, and all your hope goes down in gloom. Christ prays, because He loves so much. He prays, because the Father loves not less. Intercession is the fair fruit of their co-loving heart.

Next, see for whom this Intercession strives. Imagine a father begging for his much-loved son, a mother for her first-born child, brother for brother, friend for friend, the ardent bridegroom for his darling bride. What cries! What tears! What earnestness! What moving words! What melting arguments! What strong appeals! What fervour of desire! What bold resolve to gain the suit! But all these ties, with all their warmth, concur in Jesus. In Him there is the father's deep affection, the mother's tenderness, the brother's zeal, the friend's devoted sympathy, the bridegroom's burning love. He urges, These are My children – the travail of My soul – the offspring of My wounds – My sister – My spouse – My beloved, around whom My heart has been entwined for ever – the bride of My Father's gift, and of My loving choice – My portion – My jewels – My crown – the sheep of My pasture – My wealth – My delight – the members of My mystic body – the very apple of My eye. Such prayer is as the heart-strings strained.

Reader, are you one with Christ? Then all day long, and all time long, He wrestles thus for you.

Mark, too, how Jesus executes this office. Come, see the process of the heavenly court. Jesus appears. This is the opening act. The Spirit teaches, 'Christ is not entered into the holy places made with hands, which are the figures of the true, but into heaven itself, now to appear in the presence of God for us.' Heb. 9.24. He presents His person. The Father's eye rests on Him. Oh! with what love, what rapture, what delight! It is His son, His only begotten Son, His well-beloved Son, His elect, His beauty, His express image, His glory, His treasure, compared with whom the heavens are an empty void, and all worlds' charms a vacant nothingness. It is Jesus :– even the Servant, who has performed all His will: — who has brought all honour to His attributes: — who has ransomed all His people: — who has filled heaven with all its song. Jesus Himself appears. O my soul, your cause is in good hands.

Jesus appears. But in what form? A Lamb is seen, 'as it had been slain.' Rev. 5.6. What, then, does He show? His wounds, His bruises, His scars, His pierced hands and feet, His open side. There is no eloquence like the eloquence of a slain Redeemer. There is no argument like the argument of a God-man's death. The blood of Abel cries. Much more the blood of Jesus. Heb. 12.24. It loudly proves that the people are all bought with a worthy price, that their sins are all washed away, that their persons are all whiter than snow, that the covenant is all fulfilled, and that every grace is their purchased due. Thus Christ appears as 'He that liveth and was dead.' Rev. 1.18. O my soul, your cause is in good hands.

Jesus appears. But by what right? He comes as one whom office and duty bring. He is called and appointed and ordained to this especial work. He comes, because He must be faithful to the trust received. He comes, because it is His privilege to pass the veil. The great day in which atonement must be pleaded is arrived. The High Priest may not be absent. O my soul, your cause is in good hands.

He comes, too, with authority. He prays as one who may command. Equal addresses equal. O wondrous thought! what can the language be? 'Father, I will.' Yes! It is even so. 'Father, I will.' John 17.24. 'I will,' is God's petition to a granting God. The kingly Priest with king-like power prays. O my soul, your cause is in good hands.

He enters, too, as Advocate. As such, His Intercession has judicial force. He states the laws of the realm, the statutes of the empire, the decrees of the sovereign, the rights of the subject, the justice of the case, the demands of equity and truth. He unfolds the volume of the covenant of grace. He claims a judgment in accordance with well-counselled compact. Righteousness fails, heaven's edicts must be re-written, if such pleadings be cast out. O my soul, your cause is in good hands.

Believer, perhaps next you anxiously enquire, what is the purport of such mighty Intercession? You sigh, Oh! that I surely knew what are the blessings which He seeks for me. Draw near. His interceding voice sounds in the Gospel-page. He cried boldly and clearly from the cross, 'Father, forgive them.' He cries as boldly and as clearly from the throne, 'Father, forgive them.' As king He reigns, taking away sin. Quick as the stain defiles, He spreads His wounded hands. Pardon cannot linger. Sins and iniquities are remembered no more.

Hark! He sues again. It is, that His flock may be kept. 'Holy Father, keep through Thine own name those whom Thou hast given Me.' John 17.11. The prayer is heard. Jehovah's wings become their shield. Omnipotence defends them. Angels encamp around them. All things work to-gether for their good. Each foe is foiled. The chosen seed gets safe to heaven.

His word, too, is gone forth, 'I will pray the Father, and He shall give you another Comforter, that He may abide with you for ever, even the Spirit of truth.' John 14.16, 17. The eternal Spirit hastens to comply. He flies with con-quering wing into the willing heart. He shows the cross in its attractive glory. He shines upon the sacred page. He lifts up Jesus to the enraptured gaze. Without Christ's prayer the Spirit never comes. Without the Spirit, there is no faith, no truth, no godliness on earth.

He next gains acceptance for our prayers. What feeble babbling is our holiest worship? But answers come, sur-passing our largest hopes. How can it be? The incense of

Christ's merits fills the censer. Thus more is granted than the suppliant sought. We coldly plan, we feebly work, to magnify His name. But we succeed, and He is glorified in us. But how? His voice wins help and help we receive.

Believer, pray much. Pray more. Think whose prayers are mixed with yours. Work much – work more. Think who obtains for you the strength to prosper.

Will Christ ask more? He surely asks, until God's treasury is drained. He speaks again, 'Father, I will that they also, whom Thou hast given Me, be with Me where I am.' John 17.24. This is the summit of His love. This is the summit of His people's joy. He has no heaven without them. They have no heaven but with Him. His throne is for them. Their throne is by His side.

Believer, mark it, you must ever be with the Lord. This Intercession is the golden chain which draws and binds you to Him. It is uttered. It is continued. It is heard. It is granted. His presence is your endless heritage.

It must be so. This Intercession must prevail. Mark the ascending steps by which the Spirit leads up to the proof. Read Romans 8.34. Christ's death is full redemption. 'Who is he that condemneth? It is Christ that died.' His resurrection rises higher. It manifests in clearer light the acceptance of the finished work. 'Yea, rather, that is risen again.' His ascension soars yet higher. It crowns assurance with a heaven-high crown. 'Who is even at the right hand of God.' But Intercession reaches heights more lofty. It consummates, it perfects, it applies, it secures complete salvation. 'Who also maketh Intercession for us.' Blessed death! it reconciles. More blessed life! it much more saves. Romans 5.10. Blessed blood! it redeems. More blessed Intercession! It saves to the uttermost. Heb. 7.25. O my soul, your cause is in good hands.

Let others seek their mediators many, who are mediators none. Let others fly to intercessors many, who are intercessors none. Will not you shout that Christ is enough – 'Christ is All.'?

THE BANNER

'Moses built an altar, and called the name of it Jehovah-nissi.'
(The Lord my Banner. Marg.) *Exod. 17.15*

The fight with Amalek is past. He is given as the dust to Israel's sword, as driven stubble to his bow. Let mad assailants learn that no weapon formed against the Church of God can prosper. The arrow shot against the sun falls back upon the head. The oak rebounds upon the rending hands.

But why was sure victory on Israel's side? Because the Lord was with them. He braced the loins of their courage – they were girded with strength. He frowned – the foe can no more stand. He smiled – His people can no more fall. To whom, then, shall the praise be given? Shall worms of earth in vaunting vanity ascribe it to their worth, their counsels, the leader's leading, or the soldier's might? The thought is anguish to a pious mind. Without the Lord, what is the best man's best? He only prevails when the Lord supplies the wisdom, implants the prowess, and commands the issue. And shall not He who is the first, the last, the whole, in all success, have all the glory?

So Moses judged. He hastes to put the crown on the real Victor's head. He raises a building, not to man, but God. He adds a truthful name. He calls the altar 'Jehovah-nissi – the Lord my Banner.' This is right. This is wise. Let God have God's place – the highest of the high. Let man have man's place – the lowest of the low.

If there be baseless pretension, it is when dust claims honour, as the worker of Jehovah's works. The tool is not the agent. The pen is not the spring of thought. The labourer's spade makes not the crop to grow. The steps towards this altar give such warning.

But the structure itself is a far brighter lesson. The Spirit shows by it new features of our precious Saviour. He plainly states that the root of Jesse, David's son, is the ensign of the Redeemed. Is. 11.10. Hence, in Jehovah-nissi, faith adores Christ Jesus as its Banner.

Who hears of a Banner, and thinks not of a battle-cry? Its stand is among warrior-ranks. It tells of conflicts and of struggles. It reminds of foes assaulting, and of shocks to be sustained.

And is not the believer's hope a camp? He drinks indeed deep draughts of heavenly peace, but still the hand which takes the cup holds high the sword. His calm is like the calm of Jesus, who slept while billows tossed around. Experience proves this truth. The sandals of the Gospel are bare-worn on a battle plain. Hope rears its helmet battered by many a blow. Faith shields a heart which surely rests, but rarely knows repose. The Spirit's sword is corroded by no scabbard's rust. Can it be otherwise? Are not God's children met by an Amalek who neither dies, nor sleeps, nor spares, nor pities? This foe is Satan. His might is such, that Almightiness alone exceeds. His knowledge such, that it nears the confines of omniscience. His skill is sharpened by observance of every heart in every clime and every age. His wrath is barbed by knowing that His time is short. His hopes are plumed by slaughtered millions beneath his feet. He assails each inlet of each sense. He raises barriers before the throne of grace. No knee e'er bows but his shaft flies. He aims at every worshipper in every pew – at every hearer of the sacred truth – at every reader of the Word of God – at every hand which takes the sacramental food – at every tongue which tells of Jesu's love – at every eye which sheds the tear of penitence.

But Satan has a world to aid him. He strives to slay each man by each, and all men by all. He can paint brilliant prospects. He can raise piles of wealth. He can deck honour's crown with dazzling jewels. He sets the secret ambush. He digs the fearful pitfall. Like Heber's wife, he shows the lordly dish, but hides the hammer and the nail. Judges 4.21, 5.25.

He has fallen nature, too, on his side. There is 'the body of this death.' From this there is no fight. Self cannot separate from self. And self has a traitor's hand to introduce the foe. Self murders self, when it can work its will. Such are the troops of Amalek. But let not the believer fear. Jehovah-nissi is God's pledge, that their name shall be put out for ever. Exod. 17.14.

This Banner leads to victory. In earthly fight, the end is doubtful. The brave, the strong, may fall. The few may chase the many. Hostile hands may seize the standard. But they who cling to Christ must surely triumph. Before they strike one blow the day is won. They sally forth with conqueror's crowns, unseen indeed by eye of sense, but firmly fixed upon their brows. Do any ask how this can be? The Banner is Jehovah. All strength, all multitudes, are feeble nothingness before it. Believer, trust to your Leader, and go forward. He has led through countless conflicts, but He never lost a field. He never left a follower slain. The plains, though blood-stained, have never been the grave of faith. Each soldier may suffer much in mortifying sin. But triumph is His portion. Is it not said, 'My sheep shall never perish, neither shall any man pluck them out of my hand'? John 10.28. Jacob had many conflicts: but his aged lips bear witness to 'the Angel which redeemed me from all evil.' Gen. 48.16. David's was a struggling life, but his last song extolled a never-failing help. 'I did beat them as small as the dust of the earth; I did stamp them as the mire of the street.' 2 Sam. 22.43. Paul leaves earth with the shout, 'I have fought a good fight – henceforth there is laid up for me a crown of righteousness.' 2 Tim. 4.7, 8. Search all hell's borders. There is not one amid the lost who really fought beneath Jehovah-nissi.

The Banner is exalted. It waves high. It courts the gaze of earth. 'Go ye into all the world, and preach the Gospel to every creature.' Mark 16.15. When man fell, it was unfurled in Eden. Abel embraced it, and flew swift to heaven. Prophets and seers unfurled it more; widening hosts saw it and lived. In due time the Lord Himself appears, and plants the standard on the cross of Calvary. That was a noble eminence. That was a height which Satan could not reach. A dying malefactor discerned its clearness from the very jaws of hell, and found the gate of Paradise in dying. And from that day no sinner ever turned a longing eye to it in vain.

And now the faithful preacher's voice, the toiling missionary's love for souls, and every true disciple's holy walk, uplifts it still with ceaseless zeal. In pulpits, in heathen wilds, in filthy haunts of ignorance and vice, in thronging crowds, by dying beds, in lonely cots where sickness preys and trials vex, they cry, 'Behold Him, Behold Him.' No distance intervenes. No mists obscure. To the opened eye the beauteous Banner is both near and bright.

Believer, will you not strive by every effort, at every cost, in every place, at every moment, to make the Banner more conspicuous? Live, labour, die, pointing to it. Wave it while you can raise an arm. Earn the high glory of a standard-bearer's crown.

The Banner is attractive. It wins a willing troop. Jacob with dying gaze beheld a thronging multitude, and he bare record, 'Unto Him, shall the gathering of the people be.' Gen. 49.10. Isaiah's rapturous notes enquire, 'Who are these that fly as a cloud, and as the doves to their windows?' Is. 60.8. And He who is the Truth has pledged, 'And I, if I be lifted up, will draw all men unto Me.' So it has ever been: so it must be. There is a magnet-power in the uplifted cross. An influence subjugates the charmed mind. Its streaming scroll exhibits all which needy souls can need. The conscience-stricken sigh for ease. The guilty long for pardon. The weary and the heavy-laden seek repose. The Banner promises that beneath this standard all is yours. Here is blood to cleanse: righteousness to clothe: strength to help: mercy to pity: grace for demerit: life for death: all-sufficiency for all-deficiency. The sinner sees, believes, enlists. He cannot help but listen. Opposing friends, a sneering world, and all the wiles of Satan, are weak to stay him. Thus every day and every hour the numbers swell. And angels never cease to sing, because on earth fresh converts vow, We are the Lord's. So it shall be until heaven's army be complete.

The Banner is a worthy theme of boast. Let the vile sinner be ashamed of sin. Let the weak worldling blush at this silly world. Let unbelief hang down its childish head. Let Popery mutter its mean impostures in the dark. But let the believer with pure pride, exult in his high standard. Think – but thoughts flag – say, but words fail – what noble glories cluster here. Men boast of what is great and good and wise and lovely. Greatness! it vanishes when Christ is named. He is the mighty God. He is Jehovah's equal. He is more ancient than the eternal ages. He endures when time is gone. He spake and all worlds were. The wheels of providence subserve His will. He ever sat, and will sit, omnipotent on Omnipotence's throne. Great is the Banner. Let it be greatly praised.

Goodness! He who would learn what goodness is, must read it in the face of Christ. Is it goodness to deck nature with all things suitable to please each sense – to robe the sun with light, the air with purity, the fields with verdure, and man with faculties to enjoy? Is it goodness to look with mercy on a race undone, to lay down life to save? This is poor outline of a Saviour's goodness. Believer, boldly shout, Good is the Lord.

Wisdom! It is Christ's name. All its treasures lie hid in

Him. His plans, His work, His words, are wisdom in the highest. True wisdom never was, but as a stream from the deep fountain of His mind. Believer, wave your Banner; there is no wisdom but beside these colours.

Loveliness! The Spirit, who sees Him as He is, proclaims Him as altogether lovely. He must be lovely who is God's brightness. Mark His sweet smiles of gentle grace. Who can withdraw the admiring eye? Who can restrain the adoring tongue? Beside Him the sun hangs a black orb, and nature's charms are but a withered leaf. Sweet is it now to know Him. What will it be to see Him as He is? Let, then, faith's soldier cry aloud for joy: let him take up his manly boast before all heaven and all earth, Christ is a beauteous Banner, which surpasses praise, exceeds all worth, and soars above renown.

Believer, in conclusion, suffer an exhorting word. In every place, in every company, boldly display your Banner. Away with weak timidities. Tread down unworthy fears. Reserve is treason. Let all who know you, know Whose you are and Whom you serve. The world would tremble, unbelief would flee, if Christian warriors would rally as a compact band, 'fair as the moon, clear as the sun, and terrible as an army with Banners.' Song of Sol. 6.10. Take home this warning. Let no shame cloak your Banner.

O my soul, unfurl it in the eyes of all the scorn, and all the hate of all the world. Unfurl it in the face of all the threats and all the malice of all hell. Unfurl it – and all sins vanish, and conscience-accusations cease. Unfurl it – and the flames of hell curl back before it. Unfurl it – and heaven's portals open. Unfurl it – and you march to heaven's throne of victory.

You are now brought to the banqueting-house, where the Banner over you is love. Song of Sol. 2. 4. The palace is in sight, where the Banner over you will be glory.

MOUNT SINAI

'God spake all these words.' Exod. 20.1

Mount Sinai is not rightly seen until the Gospel-sun shine brightly on it. The total aspect then is changed. Its terrors disappear. The darkness melts into the light of life. The angry roar is hushed in notes of peace.

Reader, approach this scene with humble prayer. If the Spirit guide your steps, it will open, as a gate, to Zion's blissful slopes.

Who brings the sons of Israel to Sinai's base? It is the God of everlasting grace. His mercy looked on their enslaved estate. He burst their bonds and crushed their cruel foes. He was feeding them morn after morn with food from heaven. He was sending streams to trickle in their rear. And now, by beckoning cloud, He leads them to this spot. They may advance, then, without fear. His counsels will bud forth in blessings. This mount will be a platform to show Christ to souls. Grace must continue to be grace.

When the host reached these heights, they are addressed from heaven. Who is the speaker? The voice is that of Jesus. The Spirit clears this fact. He tells us, that the Angel, the messenger of the eternal Covenant, communed with Moses on the Mount. Acts 7.38. If Jesus speaks, the accents will be tender love. It is so here. His prelude thus brings peace into their hearts, 'Ye have seen what I did unto the Egyptians, and how I bare you on eagles' wings, and brought you unto myself.' Exod. 19.4. This preface looks not like a door to woe. It seems the first drops of a fresh shower of goodness.

An especial mandate is next heard. The Lord announces

that new revelations are at hand. Especial preparation, then, must now be made. The people are sin-soiled. Their bodies know pollution's touch. Purifying rites, therefore, must prepare them for God's approach.

Reader, you cannot learn too deeply, that 'we are all as an unclean thing, and all our righteousnesses are as filthy rags.' Is. 64.6. Do you see self as one mire-heap of filth? Do you loathe human merit as a plague-spot? Have you received the warning word, 'If I wash thee not, thou hast no part with Me?' Pause before Sinai, and weigh well your need of cleansing before you can meet God.

The third day comes. The mount is fenced. Then clouds of terror thicken. Dismay stalks forth in most appalling form. Each sight amazes, and each sound affrights. Is thunder terrible? Peal upon peal cracks in increasing roar. Are lightnings plumed with wings of swiftly-flying awe? A forked blaze pours its incessant darts. Is it a cheerless time when light is absent? Night with its blackest pall mantles the heights. Do stoutest hearts wax cold when clanging trumpets yell? Echo now maddens with their din. Was Sodom's smoking plain a frightful waste? The range of hills flares, as a murky furnace. Is it terrific to see cloud-capped summits tottering to the fall? The rocky mass now shivers as a wind-tossed reed.

But wherefore do all terrors settle on the mount? The answer is a page of solemn truth. The Spirit's mouth shall give it. 'The Lord came from Sinai, and rose up from Seir unto them. From his right hand went a fiery law for them.' Deut. 33.2. The Lord wills now to manifest His Law. The hand which holds it shakes terror over a transgressing world.

We thus are led to ask the purport of the Law. Until the soul discerns the nature of this code, God is not truly known. His Gospel is a sealed book. His holiness is an unsubstantial name.

85

The Law reveals Jehovah's majesty. It sets Him on the throne of spotless purity. It unveils the stature of His boundless righteousness. It crowns Him with the diadem, 'Holy, Holy, Holy, Lord God of Hosts.' It cries with trumpet-tongue that holiness is the pavement of His heavens, the atmosphere of His kingdom, the portals of His palace, the delight of His heart. It shows what God is, and what they must become who would appear before Him.

Where is the sinner who will now draw near without some better righteousness than self can weave? Well might Mount Sinai quake, when on its pedestal a Law like this is reared.

But was its being now first shown? Far otherwise. On creation's morn it was inwrought in Adam's heart. The parent of our race set his first steps on earth in the very likeness of the great Creator. The Maker's hand could only plant a perfect plant. Man's new-born eye thus looked unmoved on God. He trod this soil in happy innocence. His soul was purity. His voice was perfect praise. Evil was a weed unplucked. Transgression was a path untrod. Guilt was a torture yet unborn. The law of love was in each fibre of his heart. Adam thus stood. The Law was in him. He knew that to obey was life, to disobey was death.

But sinlessness soon withered in his hands. The tempter came. The tempted yielded. The beauteous fabric of the Law was shivered. Its promised life expired. Its awful curse became our heritage.

This Law, implanted in the heart of our first parents, must now be heard again on Sinai. It is God's will to show it as a written statute. Its voice, however, is the same. There is no change in its exact requirements. Its measure seems to be more vividly displayed. Its breadth and length are more distinctly marked. But its essence is all one. Two tables now contain it. Ten separate edicts open out its claims. But these brief words admit a summary more brief. The one sum of the demand is simply this – pure love. Without it none can see God's face.

But wherefore is it thus renewed? Is it God's will to cancel now the many promises which cheered the elders of the house of faith? Shall the fair page of hope, based on the blood of cleansing, be scattered to the winds? Shall Adam's race again be sent to work for life? Must their own hands erect a tower of safety from rubbish of earth's quarry?

Away with such a fearful thought! It would lead headlong to despair's foul depths. Can the poor cripple run, the broken wing expand, the withered tree bear fruit, the sentenced culprit burst his chains, the dead arise and walk? Enfeebled nature might more easily do this, than man's lost strength fulfil one mandate of the righteous Law. To send him to pluck innocence in guilt's wild wilderness, to patch a righteousness with shreds and rags of sin, to mount to heaven by a broken ladder's crumbling rounds, would be to mock his ruin and deride his woe. The Law is not republished with designs so vain.

Look steadfastly at Sinai. Amid all the terrors, angels' forms are seen. A mediator's hands receive the tables. These signs establish that grace is there. Such is the truth. God states His claims, that we, with open eye, may see our need. Our sense of ruin makes the Gospel prized. To those who have no help in self, love appears more lovely, mercy more merciful, pity more pitiful, tenderness more tender, forbearance more forbearing, God more Godlike, Christ more precious, His blood more cleansing, His righteousness more beauteous, His cross more glorious, His pardons dearer, His salvation surer, His Gospel the one home, His wounds the only refuge. Is it not grace to urge us onward towards the cross? This work is never truly done, until the Law displays God's holiness, sin's sinfulness, and hell gaping at our feet.

Satan is ever ready to persuade that a heavenly Father is too gentle to cause woe. Sinai dashes this error to the ground. It shows that God's whole nature abhors evil, and is pledged to execute just wrath. The conscious sinner looks, then, for help. There is such help in Christ, and Christ alone. Thus Sinai drives him to a Saviour's arms. This work is grace.

Sinai shows sin to be exceeding sinful and exceeding strong. In the world's school, and by deceiving lips, disguise is spread around the monster's forms. It is but faintly blamed as nature's blemish without power to hurt. But as light manifests a chamber's filth, as heat revives the frozen viper, as the sun's rays draw out the offensive vapour, as barriers cause the rushing stream to overflow, so the Law's restraints make sin to show its hideousness and giant-size. A sinner thus convinced of sin looks with horror on himself. Whither shall he flee? Jesus draws near. His blood obliterates. His grace makes free. Thus Sinai magnifies a Saviour's saving worth. This work is grace.

It is at Sinai that the Law makes bare its vengeful arm. It must have sinless purity. But if offence occur, there is no pity, there is no escape. The curse points sternly towards perdition's lake. When this is known, how precious are the sheltering arms of Jesus! Thus Sinai's truth endears the Gospel-hope. This work is grace.

Reader, has Sinai proved this Gospel-blessing unto you? If not, come now and have close dealings with it. It states its claim. You show your moral principles, your upright life, your inoffensive walk. But this is not one course of love. You start. You are undone. The thunder roars; the lightnings flash; the mountain quakes; hell is before you. But stay. This is a warning to seek help in Jesus.

You cry for mercy with imploring tears. On bended knee,

with broken heart, you sue for pardon. How vain! The Law cannot relent. No agony of grief can move its iron breast. The thunder roars; the lightnings flash; the mountain quakes; hell is before you. But stay. This is a warning to seek help in Jesus.

You urge that your transgressions were but rare, your penitence most deep, your reformation most sincere. If this were true, but true it is not, yet it cannot undo the done, or cancel what is past, or build again your fallen innocence. Oh! no. The curse must have its course. The thunder roars; the lightnings flash; the mountain quakes; hell is before you. But stay. This is a warning to seek help in Jesus.

You perhaps adduce religion's holy rites most punctually discharged. That hope, you think, will surely stand, which rests on the baptismal font, the hallowed feast, the constant service, and a strict train of unremitted forms. How good, how precious are all these, as signs of inward life, and proofs of a devoted heart! But what is their power to give unsullied righteousness? It this your best defence? The thunder roars; the lightnings flash; the mountain quakes; hell is before you. But stay. This is a warning to seek help in Jesus.

We here discern why multitudes seek peace in Rome, and Rome's poor flimsy fabric of deceits. They never saw with open eye Mount Sinai's terror. Its thunder never rolled through their awakened conscience. They know nothing of the Law's pure code. Its curse has never struck them to the ground. Their wound seems slight. A slight remedy will therefore cure. Their need seems little. Human absolution, and human sprinklings, and human prayers, will therefore make them safe. Oh! it will be dreadful to awake from such a dream, when the white throne is set, and God requires a righteousness as vast as God.

Reader, if you have fled from Sinai to the cross, this righteousness you have. Christ has fulfilled for you its utmost demand. Christ has endured for you the total of its direst curse. The Law, completely satisfied, claims heaven for you. Mount Horeb's steps exalt you to the heights of glory. Its voice of thunder hymns you to salvation's rest.

THE WILLING SERVANT

'His master shall bore his ear through with an awl; and he shall serve him for ever.' Exod. 21.6

As in nature's field, so in Israel's story, almost every object reflects Christ. Happy the hand which holds a key to open the rich treasure's door! Happy the soul which learns the art of feasting at the hallowed board! To see Christ now by faith is heaven begun. To see Christ soon in glory will be heaven complete.

The narrative before us seems at first glance to tell but a simple incident of domestic life. An Hebrew servant is the subject of the tale. His period of servitude is past. All claims have therefore ceased. He has now the option to breathe freedom's air. But freedom has no charms for him. Attachment binds him to his master's home. His dearest joys are there. His hearty language is, 'I love my master, my wife, and my children; I will not go out free.' Exod. 21.5.

A new ordinance is appointed to sanctify this willing offer of perpetual service. The judges must bear witness. An inflicted wound must also be a visible and enduring seal: 'His master shall bring him unto the judges: he shall also bring him to the door or to the door-post; and his master shall bore his ear through with an awl, and he shall serve him for ever.' Willing consent is thus proclaimed. The testifying brand is fixed. And a loved work, while life shall last, is grasped by self-devoting hands.

It may perhaps come as a new thought to some, that in this servant's choice, and in this constant love, Jesus reveals Himself. But doubts are worse than folly, when the Spirit speaks from His high seat. Read, then, the 40th Psalm. There faith ascends in heaven-high flight. It hears the eternal Son in close communion with the eternal Father. It catches these wondrous notes. 'Sacrifice and offering Thou didst not desire; Mine ears hast Thou opened,' or digged. Ps. 40.6. Jesus announces the amazing fact. Father, Mine ears are digged by Thine hand.

Here is a column of grand truth. Read it, O sons of men. Read it, my soul. Hell sees it and turns pale. Heaven sees it and resounds with praise. These words state at once, that Jesus becomes man. They speak of 'ears.' None can have these, except they wear the garments of our flesh. We have the Spirit's comment. He writes in after pages, as a co-equal clause, 'a body Thou hast prepared Me.' Heb. 10.5.

But more than this is taught. The ears are 'digged.' Here a clear finger points to the Willing Servant's pledge. We see the God-man stooping to the lowest grade. He seeks a servant's office, and a servant's toil. Jehovah's fellow is Jehovah's workman in the labour-field of grace. For God to take our nature in royal state, and on the throne of worlds, would be grace beyond all thought. But to be man in lowest bonds of servitude is grace which none but Jesus' heart can know.

We have, then, in this abject state, a speaking portrait of Christ's love. This image is the sweetest fountain of His people's peace. It is the deepest mystery set forth in simplest terms. Hence Scripture, labouring to reveal the Lord, presents the Servant's figure in repeated terms. The Father's voice announces, 'Behold My Servant, whom I uphold.' Is. 42.1. And again, 'Behold I will bring forth My Servant the Branch.' Zech. 3.8. Jesus meekly adds, 'I am among you as he that serveth.' The Spirit echoes, 'Who, being in the form of God, thought it not robbery to be equal with God: but made Himself of no reputation, and took upon Him the form of a Servant.' Phil. 2.6, 7.

He is a servant, whose time and toil are not his own. Strong obligations bind him to execute another's will.

Reader, come now and mark the service to which God calls His Son. It is to build the fabric of salvation. What strength, what zeal, what might, what wisdom, what patience, what endurance, what self-sacrifice, are needed! Survey the hindrances. In depth they reach to hell. In height they mount to heaven. Their breadth and length extend illimitable arms. A countless multitude of immortal beings lie in the vile quarry of vile sin. They must be rescued from this misery's cell. They must be made meet with all-beauteous grace. Each soul is black with stains more countless than the ocean's sands. These stains must disappear. Each owes a debt of infinite amount. This must be cancelled. Each is most justly sentenced to eternal woe. This sum of wrath must be endured. Each is weighed down beneath the Law's stern curse. This burden must be borne away. Satan has riveted his iron chains around each. These fetters must be broken off. The walls of his dark prison-house enclose them. The mighty barrier must be levelled. They are all loathsome in most filthy rags. White raiment must be wrought for them. In each the nature is estranged from God. This must be changed in every pulse and every feeling. A new heart must be implanted. Old things must pass away. Grace must commence its new-born reign. They are as scattered outcasts in a wide world's wilderness. All must be brought to hear one Shepherd's voice, and feed in one most holy fold. All must be set before the Father's throne, clear of all guilt, free from all charge, pure as God, blameless as heaven, bright as eternal day.

Such is Jehovah's gracious will. Not all the hosts of angels or of men can render aid. Deity's whole might is needed to subserve this cause.

There is a train, too, of revealing types. They must be accurately answered. There is a volume of prophetic promise. All must be fulfilled. There is a fearful catalogue of righteous threat. All must be executed. Each holy attri-

bute presents strong claims. Each must be fully satisfied
God is cast down, His empire is a broken reed, His
sovereignty is a shadow's shade, unless justice remains just
and truth continues true, and holiness shines forth inviolate
It is no easy task to render these attributes their due honour
But such is the service which must be performed.

O my soul, rejoice, be glad, give thanks, shout praises; a
willing Servant undertakes to do it. O my soul, rejoice, be
glad, give thanks, shout praises, while you draw nearer and
behold the fulfilment.

The time to work arrives. Will Jesus now draw back? I
cannot be. 'Lo, I come,' is still the language of His willing
heart. He must, then, stoop to put on human flesh. He must
be one in lowly nature with our race. He shrinks not. He
lies a babe of Adam's stock. He takes our kinsman's place
He, for whom heaven is no worthy home, is cradled, as the
meanest child of earth. Jehovah's service, man's redemption
demands descent to depths thus low.

Salvation's Servant must go slowly on through every stage
of suffering life. Be it so. It is His meat and drink to do
His Father's will. We find not one reluctant pause. He
dwells unknown in a despised town. He toils, as workman
with a workman's tools. Each cup of degradation is wrung
out.

The final scene, the bitterest effort, comes. Will Jesus
shrink? He hastens forward to meet all. Go with Him to
the garden-woe. There torturing agonies collect, which
human thought is far too weak to grasp. The sufferer stands
laden with His people's guilt. He is not spared. Wrath
rushes down with outpouring fury. He meekly bows before
the just infliction. The Willing Servant pays the whole debt
bears the whole curse, receives each crushing load, exhausts
each vial. All heaven hears the voice, 'I have glorified Thee
on the earth: I have finished the work which Thou gavest
Me to do.' John 17.4.

And now the cross is reared. The scaffold stands. Will Jesus hesitate? He is the Willing Servant to the end. Man's bitter hate drives in the nails. Hell makes its direct onset. The Father hides His smile. All earth, all heaven, desert Him. But Jesus willingly serves on, until the mightiest of all mighty words sounds forth, 'It is finished.' Yes! Salvation is accomplished. Redemption is secured. Each type is answered. Every payment is paid down. Each penalty is thoroughly endured. The curse is drained. Satan is vanquished. Hell's borders are despoiled. His people are all free. The Father's will is done, the holy service is performed, Jehovah's Servant has acted out the glorious work. 'It is finished.'

O my soul, you may indeed stand fearless on the rock of this completed service. The work is done, is fully done, is done for ever.

The heavens again receive Him. The Servant enters with a Victor's crown. There He still serves. Salvation's pyramid consists of countless stones. All must be found, and fitly framed together. They lie on many a mountain's brow, in many a hidden vale, on many a distant plain. Each is a precious soul. Each must abhor the loathsomeness of self, and joy in Jesu's blood, and cling with faith unfeigned to His saving arms.

By day, by night, without one moment's pause, Jesus pursues the work of winning souls. He sends His Spirit on the wings of love. He calls and qualifies subserving ministers. At His command they raise the beacon of the cross. Devoted missionaries break all endearing ties, and seek the outcasts beneath tropic suns, in ice-clad rocks, and amid tribes which Satan holds in death-cold bonds.

Thus Christ still serves the purposes of grace. A mighty voice cries, Come. And all who are ordained to life obey. Onward the healing waves will roll until the blessed company is complete. Then comes the end. The glorious plan

95

is gloriously finished. The kingdom is delivered to the Father. The Willing Servant shows the collected mass all gathered in, all saved. Not one is lost. Not one is absent. Each member of the mystic body fills its place.

Reader, at that day where will be your place? Oh! pause. Put not the question from you. Perhaps you sigh, I would be numbered with the saved, but how can I have hope? Tell me. Where is your fear? Is it lest the tremendous billows of your sins should swell above His willingness to save? If all the guilt of all the lost multiplied and magnified beyond all power to count or measure, weighed heavily upon your conscience, still venture to His feet. The willing Jesus will not cast you out. His heart, His love, His zeal, His pity, His bleeding wounds, His undertaken office, all forbid. Let not His acts on earth, let not His voice from heaven, be in vain. Did misery ever seek relief from Him, and not receive more than a ready welcome?

Fly forth in spirit to the bright saints in light. The testimony from each rejoicing heart is one. They all give glory to a willing Jesus.

With united voice they tell, that when they cast their ruined souls upon Him, He tenderly embraced, and sweetly cheered, and fully pardoned, and entirely saved.

Hear now His voice. Throughout the Bible, and from faithful lips, it still is sounding – Wilt thou – Wilt thou be made whole?

Be then persuaded. Tarry not. Let this accepted moment find you a willing suppliant at a willing Saviour's cross. None ever perished because Christ would not hear. None ever fell into the burning lake because He turned from the beseeching cry.

But stay, there is another word. It seals perdition on all who stand apart. Take heed, lest it enclose you in its hopeless doom. 'Ye will not come to me, that ye might have life.' John 5.40.

THE ARK OF THE COVENANT

'They shall make an ark.' Exod. 25.10

Reader, come see the chiefest wonder of the wondrous Tabernacle. It is the Ark. For this the holy tent was reared. For this the holiest place was set apart. This is the richest jewel of the sacred casket, the topstone of the hallowed pile.

Its form was first displayed in heaven. God gave the plan to Moses. In heaven it still is visible to faith. John saw it with enraptured eye. We read, 'The temple of God was opened in heaven, and there was seen in His temple the Ark of His testament.' Rev. 11.19.

All this exhibits Christ. He is the Ark of redemption, the scheme of which was drawn above. In fulness of time it was set up below. And now it shines, and ever shall shine, the glorious glory of the new Jerusalem.

When God describes the holy vessels, observe, this takes precedence. He first shows that which shows His Son most clearly. It is His will that Christ should be set forth without a cloud, in full-orb splendour. May the same mind be ours! May He fill up the foreground of each thought and work! Let no reserve, let no unworthy veil obscure the brightness of His brightest smile. God puts the glories of His First-born first. Woe to the man who hides Him in the rear!

The Ark is a plain chest. Its length is less than four feet. Its height and breadth are scarcely more than two. Jesus is simple majesty. He needs no art to decorate His grace. It is impure and pitiable taste which craves for outside show.

The substance of the Ark is wood. This proves an earthly birth. Trees spring from this our lower soil. Here Jesus is portrayed the woman's Seed – the kinsman of our race. O my soul, ponder more and more Christ's visit to our low abode. He takes our prison rags, that He may bear our prison woe. He becomes man, that with man's lips He may exhaust our cup of wrath. Christ's sufferings in the flesh leave us no sufferings to pay.

This is no common wood. Corruption cannot soil it. It defies decay. So human nature, as put on by Christ, is human nature without spot of sin. It is a lovely sight to see man treading earth, and no mire cleaving to the feet; and breathing our polluted air, without infection's taint.

The Ark is more than wood. Its every part is covered with pure gold. This metal, put over the coarse case, shows that our Jesus is much more than man. Grand truth! Sing, O ye heavens, and rejoice, O earth. The lowly Saviour is the mighty God. Vain were the wounds, the blood, the agony, the death, unless the merit have a boundless worth. One soul which never sinned might buy one sinning soul from curse. But Jesus satisfies for multitudes, many as the sea-shore grains, and countless as the stars of night. His Deity enables. His every act and every pain is measureless as God can be. Infinite deaths are died upon His cross. Infinite obedience is wrought out in His life. O my soul, look often at the Ark. It witnesses that Christ is very man, a spotless man, and man conjoined with perfect Deity and so the Saviour whom your case requires.

A crown surrounds the summit. This speaks of kingly state. And is not Christ a king? The Father's voice decides it; 'Yet have I set My King upon My holy hill of Zion.' Ps. 2.6. The Spirit cries aloud, 'He hath on His vesture and on His thigh a name written, KING OF KINGS, AND LORD OF LORDS.' Rev. 19.16. Who will not add, Lift up your heads, O portals of my heart, and let the King of Glory enter in? Happy they, who give Him the throne of every thought, and crown Him daily with high crowns of praise! Let the ungodly pierce Him with mockery's thorns. Reader, place on His brow the jewel of your ransomed soul.

Coffers are made to hold some treasure. They have the custody of precious things. That surely, then, must be a priceless prize, which shall be guarded within walls like these. And so it is. The Ark receives the Tables of the Law. God had revealed His will. He had drawn on a chart His own transcendant holiness. This transcript of the eternal mind was folded in this chest. Now look to Christ. He is the Law-containing Ark. The Spirit, not the letter, dwells in Him. The world reviled this code. Man cast it from him. Christ gave Himself to be its sacred home. He hid it in the chambers of His breast. Hear His appeal, 'I delight to do Thy will, O My God! yea, Thy law is within My heart.' Ps. 40.8. Christ is embodied Law.

Next, the Ark is covered. A lid of solid gold is placed for especial purpose, and with especial name. The purpose is to hide the Law from every eye. This brings us to the glorious work of Christ. The Law has a stern voice. Mark its requirements. They are very long and very wide. Their breadth embraces the whole of each man's life. They rigidly exact obedience, without one falter or one flaw. Mark, too, its curse. It has one fearful threat. Eternal ruin is transgression's doom. Christ comes to hide these terrible demands. He spreads Himself along the vast dimensions of the requiring and the condemning code. His life is satisfaction to the whole. So, too, He bears its utmost penalties. He suffers till its wrath can take no more. God looks upon His Son. He finds obedience rendered and the curse endured. An exact covering conceals all claims. No part appears to ask for further dues.

The lid has an especial name. It is the Mercy-seat. We now are taught why pure gold, without any admixture, is its substance. Mercy has no birth-place but in heaven. It yearns, indeed, over our fallen race. It speeds, indeed, to earth. But its high origin is far above. Hence nothing but pure gold, God's emblem, can form this Mercy-seat. It is a

99

fitting name. For what is mercy, but Christ in His finished work? Christ is the ocean, in which every drop is infinite compassion. He is the mountain towering above mountains, in which every grain is God's own goodness. He is the mirror of God's loving heart, the pinnacle of tender grace. O my soul, know the full comfort of the Mercy-seat. When your short-comings fill you with dismay, see Christ – your mercy – spreading His own robe around you; when threatening thunders peal, seek safety in His covering side. Bless Jesus more and more. His mercy shelters. His mercy saves. His mercy endures for ever.

Can more be added to the Ark? Faith fain would see some token of redeemed souls. It looks again. Nor looks in vain. At either end a cherub has its place. No foreign metal frames this glittering pair. They and the Mercy-seat are of one piece. Aloft they spread their wings, thus shadowing the lid. Their faces turn towards each other, but look intently on the seat below. Reader, come learn some obvious lessons from these mystic forms. They rest upon the Mercy-seat. The heirs of life have no dependence but on Christ. On Him they lean for every help. On Him they cast the burden of their sins. 'Other foundation can no man lay, than that is laid, which is Jesus Christ.' 1 Cor. 3.11.

They are, too, part and parcel of the Lord. He is the Head – they are the members. One sap pervades the stem and branch. Christ's Spirit animates each fibre of the Church. All are 'partakers of the divine nature.' 2 Pet. 1.4.

Their expanded wings proclaim their readiness for instant work. The cry of grateful love is always one: 'Lord, what wilt Thou have me to do?' Speak but the word, and swiftly I will fly. My plumes delight to speed in Thy behalf.

They turn towards each other. Oneness of purpose, oneness of heart, oneness of action, is the pure mark of God's pure sons. They look not to their own, but to the common weal. Without diverging glance, in harmony and love, they seek the glory of their glorious Lord.

But every eye is riveted on Christ. They dwell with prying gaze on the mysteries of the Mercy-seat. They have no look for other objects, nor mind for other knowledge. Their sigh is, Oh! that we might know Him more and more, and see with clearer view the wonders of His person, His grace, His love, His work. The more they search the more they learn. The more they learn the more they crave. Eternity must end before the end of Christ be reached.

A promise, bringing heaven down to earth, surmounts the whole. God adds, 'There will I meet with thee, and I will commune with thee from above the Mercy-seat.' Exod. 25.22. The anxious soul will often breathe the longing thought, 'Oh! that I knew where I might find Him.' Reader, there is no doubt. The spot is fixed. Come to the Mercy-seat. There God is present to hear, to answer, and to bless. There He will open all His heart, and deal as friend with friend, in all the freeness of familiar love. Then linger not. Plead Christ, your law-fulfilling righteousness. Claim Christ, your law-appeasing victim. Show Christ as 'set forth of God to be a propitiation,' or Mercy-seat, 'through faith in His blood.' Rom. 3.25. As you draw near, God will draw near to you. In Christ you come. In Christ He meets you. The Mercy-seat joins you to God. The Mercy-seat joins God to you.

Will any say that the Ark of Moses is no more? True. When the Temple fell, this framework disappeared. But Christ, the substance, ever lives. In heaven the Throne of Grace cannot be moved. The name is changed, but the reality is one. Material forms are lost. Essential blessings have eternal life. Yes! While needs lasts we may go boldly to a ready throne. God waits with open hand. With open hand His people take. O my soul, pass often through the parted vail. You will return laden with mercies, rich in grace, refreshed with heavenly converse, and made meet for a heavenly home.

Moreover, the Ark had staves. By these the priests conveyed it. It was the constant centre of the marching host. It moved or tarried as they moved or stayed. Thus Christ abides, the inmate of the faithful heart. At home, abroad, in solitude, in work, indwelling Deity gives dignity and peace.

The staves might not be taken out. They kept their place in readiness for instant movement. It is true that Christ never finally deserts His own who once have welcomed Him. But let them watch and pray, and hold Him fast with clinging love and fervency of zeal. For if the world creeps in, and rival lusts are fondled, His gracious smile will cease to cheer, His precious presence will seem to vanish.

Let congregations, too, and churches fear. The staves give warning, that departure may be near. The Gospel comes. It calls. It is not heeded. What then? It passes on, and may be no more heard. The true Light has shone on many a spot which now is dark as death's dark vale.

Reader, let not the Ark thus speak to you in vain. Receive it, prize it, and Obed-edom's blessings will enrich you. 2 Sam. 6.11. Enshrine it in your heart. Then all strongholds of sin, like Jericho, will fall before it. The idols of self-righteous forms will lie, like shivered Dagons, at its feet. And when you reach the stream of Jordan, Christ, the true Ark, will lead you onward, and parting waters will be your passage to the land of rest.

THE TABLE OF SHEW-BREAD

'Thou shalt also make a table.' Exod. 25.23

Reader, have you passed the threshold of the home of grace? Is soul-death behind you? Is soul-life your portion? If so, you daily hunger for divine repast. The proof of life is sure. The new-born craves for food. And no food satisfies, but Christ Himself.

These lines are written to commend such feast. A Table here is spread, of which the whole provision is Christ's person and Christ's work. The saints of old found their abundance here. Yet there is more. The banquet still is rich. The Spirit's call is ever heard, 'Eat ye that which is good, and let your soul delight itself in fatness.' Is. 55.2.

Our gracious God directs, 'Thou shalt also make a Table of shittim-wood, and overlay it with pure gold.' Observe this. The thought and plan are wholly from above. It is no human pattern or design. God loved, God willed, God spake. As Christ is the offspring of free grace, so grace contrives each image which reveals Him.

In height it is co-equal with the Ark. The measure of its length and breadth is less. Its substance is identically one. The inward frame is that choice wood, of which the virtue could resist all taint. The outside shines in the chaste splendour of pure gold.

Reader, revolve the precious teaching of these chosen signs. Their terms are plain. They show the redemption-wonder. Wood is conjoined with gold. This is poor manhood taken into God. This is the Godhead linked to our mean flesh. God remains God, and yet is man. Man remains man, and yet is one with God. Such is our Jesus,

103

moving, working, dying, upon earth. Such is our Jesus, sitting, working, reigning, in the heavens.

Reader, let ceaseless praises prove that your gratitude discerns this truth. Cry out and shout – Christ is man; His doings are put down as mine. Christ is God; His doings must suffice.

The Table is well-stored. Christ is the richness of all rich supply. Count all the drops of ocean, and all the grains which form our globe, and all the rays, which pour down from the sun. They are mean scantiness compared with Him. View other boards. The dainties of the world are choking dust. The hungry eat, and hunger bites with sharper tooth. Self is a barren waste. No soul of man can reap refreshment in that blighted field. The mere outside of forms and rites is unsubstantial as the passing cloud. Many, indeed, apply; but disappointment mocks them all. The same is true of every board but Christ. He is the one abundance which abounds for ever. He is the one full Table which is ever full.

But what is the supply? It is bread. 'Thou shalt set upon the Table Shew-bread before Me always.' Exod. 25.30. Faith knows this emblem well. It has often sat in rapture at the feet of Jesus, and heard His own lips say, 'I am the bread of life.' It knows, too, the reviving taste. It has found Christ to be its staff of strength, the healthful juice of its exhausted powers.

But bread is formed of grain, which earth brings forth, and labour grinds, and culinary process kneads, and oven's heat completes. Christ is all this. He is bone of our bones, flesh of our flesh. The heavy burden of man's sins bruised Him to powder, crushed Him to the grave. All hell put forth its art to sift Him as the wheat is shaken. And all the flames of God's wrath blazed fiercely round Him. Thus He became the Bread of God – the saving food of souls.

Will any meal avail to make this consecrated mass? What

saith the Lord? 'Thou shalt take fine flour.' Lev. 24.5. No unclean grain, no refuse husk, no worthless chaff, can taint this holy lump. All its material is pure perfection. Here is Christ's manhood, as free from evil as God's life can be. This truth is precious. The anxious soul will often ask, May I lie down and die, without one fear, on Christ? The Spirit uses sword after sword to slay each doubt. He testifies by frequent word, in frequent type, that sin could no more touch Him, than man's hand can reach God's throne, or soil the sun with stains.

A name distinguishes this food. It is called Shew-bread The term implies Bread of faces, or Bread of presence. There is a length of truth wound up in Bible-titles. As we unfold them, there seems to be no end. We here are taught that this Bread was spread forth before Jehovah's face, laid out in His immediate presence. This is an emblem of our Lord. There never has been moment in which He lived not the darling of the Father's eye. There never can be. He says, 'Before the worlds were framed, I was by Him, and I was daily His delight, rejoicing always before Him.' Prov. 8.30. God viewed Him, then, as the one centre of His heart's desire. And never can His eye stray from Him. He views Him still with loving gaze, as having executed all His purposes of grace, as having magnified His name beyond all honour, as having vindicated the majesty of truth and jus- tice. All that God is, finds sweet refreshment in this Presence-bread.

The number of the loaves is fixed. They must be twelve. 'Thou shalt set them in two rows, six on a row, upon the pure Table before the Lord.' Lev. 24.6. There is sweet meaning in this gracious rule. The twelve express the tribes of Israel. Each has allotted place on the presenting board. These classes had their differing marks. In size, in wealth, in promises, in privilege, in heritage, their state was diverse.

But here not one is overlooked: not one is put aside. The Table sets all equally in order before God.

The numbered tribes are a clear picture of the numbered Church. Hence every child of faith is present in the Presence-bread. They all are members of the Lord. They all in Him appear before the Father's eye. Degrees of faith may vary. Some may but touch with trembling hand the very edge of Jesus' garment. Others may live with their enraptured head upon His very breast. But if there be vital faith, there is an oneness with the Lord which never, never can be parted. Christ holds each one within Himself. He shows Himself the compound of them all. They lived in Him. They died in Him. They rose in Him. They sit together in heavenly places in Him. God's look, which rests upon His Son, sees them. The love which smiles on Jesus smiles on them.

Believer, whatever be your need, your misery, your sense of sin, your loathing of vile self, turn to the Table of Shew-bread. Your image there is comely. Christ lives to represent you. While God delights in Him, He must delight in you. He ever sees you wrapt up in His Son.

The Bread received a crown upon its summit. The crown was frankincense. Thus constant fragrance shed delight around. Christ is sweet savour. The sin-removing blood, the interceding prayer, the spotless righteousness, the incense of the finished work, are heaven's own myrrh.

O my soul, is Christ this frankincense to you? You hear the voice, 'This is My beloved Son, in Whom I am well pleased.' Is there the glad response, This is my beloved Saviour: in Him, I am indeed well pleased?

On the return of every Sabbath morn, the priests brought fresh supplies. At no moment was the Table void. Ye ministers of Christ, mark well this fact. It is a sign which teaches you how you must teach your flocks.

The Sabbath hours are golden time. The pulpit opens to

you. Assembled crowds hang on your lips. The hungry press round you to be fed. What bread do you produce? No food can satisfy which is not Christ. This must be gathered in the fair fields of Scripture, where nothing grows but holiest grain. It must be sifted with most anxious search. It must be worked upon the knees. It must be turned with agonizing prayer. It must be always new, but always one. Its savour must be only Christ.

The Presence-bread was still the same in substance and in form – but newly placed and newly prepared for its sacred use. O Sirs, look well to this. A dwindled and decaying flock might move angelic hosts to tears. But dwindle and decay they must, if the bread be poison or if the food be stale. Woe to the preacher who thus sins! There can be no excuse. The Bible is before him. It is a storehouse in which Christ is All – and ever new. Will he not take that he may give? Will he not give that he may save from death? Hark to the moan of many a famished soul; I starve; this food is Christless. I starve; this food is tasteless.

The Bread removed became the priests' repast. Within the holy place they ate the holy food. There is especial care for those who do especial work. And why? They have especial need. Such is the pastor's case. What cares oppress! What toils exhaust! What anxious days and nights beat down! But Jesus calls him to the secret chamber of His presence, and feeds him with the first-fruits of His truth. Thus with new power he runs anew his sun-like course. But woe, indeed, to him who shows a Saviour whom he has never seen, and preaches Christ from Christless heart, with Christless lips. O Sirs, there is a voice from Balaam's bed of fire, there is a wail from the low cell of Judas, which warns with an appalling note. Let none take Christ upon the preaching lip, who do not feed on Him with ravished heart.

But here is food for the whole family of faith. In Gospel-day, the lowest servant is a priest of God. Rev. 1.6. Hence, all are welcomed to the Presence-bread. Children of grace, know your high privilege. The board with all its treasures is for you. Look to the Presence-bread again. It tells you what is the true act of faith. Is it enough to hear of food? Is it enough to see, to smell, to touch? Oh! no. Hearing and sight remove no hunger and supply no strength. To gain support, the lips must taste, the food must circulate throughout the frame. So Christ must be received in all His grace, in all His truth, into each fibre of the heart and soul. He must be present in the inner man, life of our life, strength of our strength, health of our health, joy of our joy.

Reader, is your soul craving thus for Christ? Is it thus feasting on Him? He is before you. You have not far to seek. Faith can receive at any moment and in any place. It cries, 'Lord, evermore give us this bread' – and as it cries, it takes – and as it takes, it joys – and as it joys, it blesses – and as it blesses, it takes more, and strengthens more, and shows its greater strength in greater labours and in louder praise.

But perhaps you care nothing for this Table of Shew-bread. May God the Spirit in mercy lead you to it! Hark! He cries, 'Come, for all things are now ready.' Will you refuse? Remember Eve. The tempter showed her the forbidden fruit. How easily she yielded; how quickly she took! He now shows you the husks, and rubbish of the world. Will you be as easily enticed? Sin touched, sin tasted, sin digested, is hell and all hell's pains. But come to this Table. Take Christ, love Christ, feed daily, hourly, on Christ – and yours is the fulness of joy now, and all heaven's blessedness for ever.

THE GOLDEN CANDLESTICK

'Thou shalt make a Candlestick of pure gold; of beaten work shall the Candlestick be made.' Exod. 25.31

Reader, in holy thought enter the holy Tent. You pass a curtain rich in richest hues. Then what a scene appears! Light in its loveliest softness gleams around. The pure-gold sides, the pure-gold vessels, the sparkling canopy, the cherubied vail cast back resplendent rays.

Whence flows this tide of day? The orbs of heaven lent not their aid. No sun-gleam plays, no moon-beam sleeps upon the radiant walls. A Candlestick alone lifts high a seven-crowned head: and night is no more known.

Faith looks, and soon discerns the truth of the bright vessel. Glad memory recalls the word, 'The city had no need of the sun, neither of the moon, to shine in it, for the glory of God did lighten it, and the Lamb is the light thereof.' Rev. 21.23. It sees that this must be an image of that heavenly home in which Christ is the full light. The light, then, here exhibits Him. Christ is the seven-lamped Candlestick.

It is so. All is darkness without Him.

Let us now pause, and trace with humble prayer the beauties of this Gospel-portrait. Holy Spirit, we would see Jesus. Wilt not Thou reveal Him? No heart of man can learn, except Thy teaching voice go forth.

First, what shall be brought to form a stand which shall prefigure Christ? Our costliest wealth seems mean for such high use. Value is valueless beside Him. But earth can only give her purest substance. It is pure gold. This is the metal, then, which God, the great artificer, selects.

Reader, this choice proclaims that Christ is an all-gold

Saviour. Yes! There is no dross, no flaw, no blemish in Him. Mark well His blood. Oh! wondrous truth. It is divine. Divinely it weighs down all mountains of vile sin. Divinely it pays all claims of infinite demands. Divinely it sets free the debt-bound of a countless family. Divinely it satisfies, till satisfaction overflows.

Gaze on His righteousness. It also is divine. God's eye can never joy in it enough. God's throne can scarcely give it worthy seat. This decks the Church in spotless robe. 'The King's daughter is all glorious within: her clothing is of wrought gold.'

Give ear to His unfailing prayer. Its incense is perpetual fragrance. Its power moves the heart of God. It cannot ask in vain. Thus golden blessings bless the ransomed race.

Next, the pure gold is beaten. Fast-falling blows batter it to shape. This image leads us to the stricken Jesus. Redemption is an agonizing work. It cost but little to form countless worlds. It costs but little to sustain them. God willed, and they shone forth. He wills, and they still shine. But torments without limit must be borne to free one soul from sin's dues.

My soul, oft ponder this amazing truth. Your sins are many as all ocean's sands. Each is most justly doomed to all the fury of most righteous wrath. God hates your evil, and is pledged to punish. Truth dies if sin escapes. In person or by proxy you must take its curse. But Jesus is this proxy. He 'suffers, the just for the unjust.' He pleads: I come to represent a sentenced culprit. Spare him, and pour all punishment on Me. God in His grace consents. Wound follows wound, till in the deepened grave of scars, all guilt is buried from His sight.

But O my soul, your case is only one. Salvation's roll has names which baffle number. For each, for all, Christ bears all woe. He shrinks not, till the last sin of His last child is fully washed out by His bleeding stripes. Thus Christ is bruised. Thus the pure gold is beaten. The anvil and the hammer of inflicted blows work out a perfect Saviour.

The gold is beaten into beauteous form. A luxury of ornaments decks every part. The branches shine as clustered trees of fruit and flowers.

Reader, we thus are led to mark the full-blown loveliness of Christ. Say, what is beauty? Is it not the union of symmetric charms? Is it not a matchless harmony, in which each part adds grace to each? Is it not a power which rivets gaze, and chains each sense in fetters of delight, and makes the mind a flood of ecstacy?

Then what is beauty but Christ Jesus? Survey His person. It is our manhood decked in glorious Deity. It is a lustre which outshines the sun. It is a fairness beside which the heavens look black. It is the statue for which eternal counsels cannot raise a pedestal too high.

Survey His work. It is exact proportion. All claims of God, all need of man have their just place. It is a pyramid based in eternal love, and crowned with eternal glory. Each stone is a saved soul. Each is the mirror of Jehovah's greatness.

They who, through grace, thus see their Lord, never withdraw their love. Their hearts are fixed. The beauties of Christ eclipse all other charms. This is the delight of Scripture. Christ beautifully shines in every page. This is the sweet relish in each Gospel-ordinance. Christ is enjoyed, the savour of the whole. Hence springs the longing to depart. To die is to meet Christ face to face.

The central stem sends forth six branches from its sides. It thus presents the image of a spreading tree. And such is Christ. At Calvary a little seed is cast into the soil. But soon the vigorous sprouts appear. The boughs go forth into all lands and distant nations find luxuriant shade. What though this earth is most uncongenial to the plant! Still it thrives and blossoms and bears fruit: and grateful foliage screens reposing crowds.

Reader, is your calm seat beneath this shelter? Is your soul-feast from these soul-feeding tendrils? If it be not so, what is your hope? where your excuse? You cannot say that Christ's arms spread not above your dwelling. Open your eye and behold Him. Stretch out your hand and touch Him. If you refuse, you perish. And it is sad death to die beneath the tree of life.

The seven-fold branches support seven-fold lamps. Each summit is a coronet of fire. Little would be the profit of the costly frame, unless light sparkled from it. But it burns brightly. This is its especial purpose. The mystic number and the constant blaze show Christ a perfect and unfailing light.

Study this first-born of creation's gifts. It is the life, the joy, the grace of nature's world. And is not Christ the life, the joy, the grace of the poor sinner's soul?

Without this inmate, where is the Tabernacle's splendour? Its brilliant colours are all colourless. Its golden walls are a dark blank. All form, all shape, all rays are the black sameness of a vault. The eye looks round on undistinguishable night.

Without the sun, where are creation's charms? The trees hang down their withered heads; the meadows are a noxious swamp; the melody of groves is hushed; the skies above frown as a pall of adamant; the earth's flowery carpet is an icy rock; death shivers on a frozen throne.

Such is man's heart, without the light of Christ. It is a poisoned marsh, a barren desert, a joyless waste, a rayless night, a deathful tomb. It must be so, because God is unknown. The great Jehovah is love and grace and mercy and tender pity and power and wisdom and truth and holiness and justice. But where is this discerned? What is the high school of such high thought? Nature cannot teach this. It is not written in the page of providence. The law shows nought but angry frowns. Reason's poor taper only cheats. Unaided wisdom, with its strongest wing, can only flutter in the vale of vanity. No earth-born eye can catch a glimpse of God.

But let the Sun of Righteousness arise; let Christ send forth His heaven-bright rays. Then the scene changes. Then what floods of glory roll the mists away! The face of Jesus shows the truth of God. Each attribute is seen in Him as the clear blue of heaven. All then appear entwined in harmony's embrace, taking delight in bringing in salvation, and glorifying God in glorifying man. Behold the cross. A halo round about it writes in golden letters: God hates sin, and loves the sinner. He is just, and justifies the ungodly. He is righteous, and passes by unrighteousness. He is holy, and makes fit the unholy for His kingdom. He is free grace, and peoples heaven from lost souls. He is glory, and builds His glorious palace from the mire of earth's quarry. Christ, Christ alone, shows this. Christ, then, is Light.

Without Christ, too, the matters of this world are but a puzzled maze. Poor blinded man sees nothing as it really is. He knows not the true end of being. He takes the tinsel to be gold. He counts the gold as dross. He treasures up the chaff as wheat. He casts the precious grain as playthings to the wind. All his view is bounded by time's narrow line. All his heart is fixed on vanity's vain trifles. He chases bubbles on perdition's brink. He profits no one and he ruins self.

The case is different when Christ shines inward. The opened eye then clearly sees the purpose and the end of being. The Bible-lamp then shows that man's true object is to win salvation. Wisdom then cries: Seek pardon for transgression, pleas for remission, acquittal at the judgment bar, and hope beyond the grave. The Gospel-torch reveals the mighty fact that space is granted to gain grace. Christ brings man to this clear-day life. Christ, then, is Light.

Reader, is He the Candlestick within your soul? Then see that its pure blaze ascends. It was the priest's part to trim and dress it every morn. It had golden implements to remove the dross and to revive the flame. And golden implements are ready for your hand. You know them well. Oh! use them rightly, and with pious zeal. Prayer, meditation, Scripture-ordinances, holy communion, holy labours, are golden tools for this most sacred work. God ordained means to tend these lamps. He provides helps to fan the flame within you.

It may be that you sometimes sit in the dark chamber of distress and doubt and fear. Your light is dim. But why? The fault is not with Christ. He is still near, and ready to shine forth. Arise! Apply the oil which the Spirit brings. In prayer before the Gospel-page, stir up the fading embers. Brightness will soon re-appear, and cheering rays make gladness more glad.

Is there a reader whose heart is not the tabernacle of these lamps? Ah! Sir, your case indeed is sad. Your eyes have never seen that lovely sight which is the joy of heaven and earth. Gross darkness covers you, but thicker night awaits you. But hark! A wondrous word calls after you. Oh! that it might rise as Bethlehem's star, to guide you to the Saviour! Oh! that it might be the first ray of salvation's orb! Hark! it cries, 'Awake, thou that sleepest, and arise from the dead, and Christ shall give thee light.' Eph. 5.14. Christ is the giver and the gift. Christ is the enlightener and the light. May you receive! May you reflect!

THE TABERNACLE

'Moreover thou shalt make the Tabernacle.' Exod. 26.1.

The worship of the living God was well known to Israel's sons. They had raised altars to His name. The slaughtered victim and the curling smoke had oft declared acquaintance with the way of peace. In holy rites, at many a blood-stained stone, their faith had used the ordered means.

But till they reached the base of Sinai, no stated house for stated service had been reared. Here first the gracious word went forth, 'Let them make Me a sanctuary, that I may dwell among them.' Exod. 25. 8. Here mercy planted the earliest symbol of God's constant presence. Here earth received her eldest model of a consecrated fane.

Happy the day throughout the camp when this Tent showed its new-born head. What thrilling joy would beat in every heart? What anxious scrutiny would scan each part! Reader, draw near in spirit. Take your stand amid the wondering crowd. Admire with them the progress of the work.

First, a measure-line is drawn. The length extends to forty-five feet: the breadth to fifteen. Solid foundations then are placed. A belt of silver sockets is laid down. Into this base the sides are fixed. These much exceed in preciousness. They are composed of choicest wood, and clad in purest gold. Their height ascends to fifteen feet. Especial care conjoins the corners. And bars of gold stretch out their binding arms, to make the walls secure. Five shining pillars guard the eastern entrance. Rich drapery thence hangs. Such is the outward frame. Four pillars rise within, to separate an inner chamber. These pillars hold a vail of costly work, to screen the Holiest from all view. This room is fifteen feet in each extent. The breadth, the length, the height, are one in uniform dimension. The house thus shaped is covered by four curtains. The first is wrought with brilliant hues, and sparkles with cherubic forms. A starry canopy thus vaults the roof. This is defended by a pure white vest. Next, a stronger skin of red is spread. The outward garment is a coarse sheet of rough material. This last completes the structure.

Such is the front which meets the eye. But mark, God willed the gracious boon. He drew the plan. He gave the model. He inspired the skill. Each part, then, is His wisdom. Each has a Gospel-tongue. Each heard aright reveals that 'Christ is All.' This is not fancy's dream. It is the Spirit's clear-toned lesson. He cries to all the family of faith: Look to the Tabernacle, and behold your Lord. There is a pulpit from which no voice is heard but His. It is the Bible. Its pages teach, 'We have such an High Priest, who is set on the right hand of the throne of the Majesty in the heavens; a Minister of the sanctuary, and of the true Tabernacle, which the Lord pitched, and not man.' Heb. 8.1, 2. This earthly Tabernacle, then, is but a sketch of that fair frame of Christ, which God, the Holy Spirit, wrought and planted in this earth. Again, like testimony sounds in Heb. 9.11: 'Christ being come an High Priest of good things to come, by a greater and more perfect Tabernacle, not made with hands, that is to say, not of this building.' The word is plain. The Tabernacle points to a mystic fabric, which human hands produce not, which human skill erects not, which human imperfection taints not. What can this be but Christ in the flesh, but not of flesh? Surely all doubts take wing. Divine authority decides the fact. Christ is discerned, the end and excellence of the predictive house.

Reader, pursue the clue thus found: and steep your soul in depths of heaven-born truth. View through this glass the various parts.

Bright silver forms the base. Whence comes this wealth? By whom and with what purpose is it given? It is the ransom-price of souls. Each numbered child of Israel brought a redemption-sum. It was a silver coin. Wealth might not add, nor poverty subtract. Exod. 30.12 – 16. This holy tax supplied the base. Exod. 38.27.

My soul, what lessons cluster here! We see how sin destroys, how grace redeems. Our liberty is gone, our life is lost. A tyrant claims us. Justice demands its dues. But Jesus is laid low. The earth drinks in His blood. His merits are our ransom-price. His death is ransom paid. The Father testifies content: 'Deliver him from going down to the pit, I have found a ransom.' Job 33.24. The sockets add the echo of their proof. The Gospel-structure rests on a ransom. Remove it, and redemption falls. Without a price, the Saviour has no saved. But the foundation is most sure. The Tabernacle firmly stands. Our Gospel-sockets never can be moved.

Next mark what splendid boards are tightly fastened to these pure supports. Two substances are here combined. They show a double nature: and thus proclaim the Incarnate God. Yes! Christ is here in Deity's transcendent blaze, in manhood's spotless purity. O my soul, how great, how meet is your redeeming Lord! All power is His to rescue and to satisfy, for what can resist the boundless might of God? Fitness is His to take your place. He bears your flesh. He wears your form. This is the fact which wins for Him salvation's throne. This is the truth on which faith lives and joys and dies and soars to glory. Hence, types prefigure it, and prophets sing it and Gospel narrative records it. Hence, at each step of Jesus' life, the Spirit points, Behold the man – Behold the God! A babe is cradled in a manger-bed, while wondering angels announce 'Christ the Lord.' A mean abode scarce shelters the young child; while a new star brings distant sages to His feet. He sleeps as weary man; He arises as the mighty God, and stills the raging storm. He sits a worn-out traveller by the well, but speaks eternal life to a dead sinner's soul. He weeps in human sympathy at the grave but utters the sovereign mandate, 'Lazarus, come forth.' He moves about as lowliest of our lowly race: but at His word, dumb sing, lame leap, blind see, deaf hear, the weeping smile, each malady departs, and homes of anguish brighten with delight. As dying worm, He hangs upon the cross: as Lord of life and glory, He snatches a poor lost one from the jaws of hell. As a weak corpse, the tomb receives Him. As conqueror of the grave, He strides forth in the strength of God. As friend, He gives last counsels to His friends: as God He mounts to heaven's high throne. Thus Scripture labours to fix the deep truth, that a God-man redeems us.

O my soul, grasp tight the tidings. In face of sin and guilt and death and hell and judgment, cry out and shout, Christ is my All, for He is God: Christ is my All, for He is God in my own form. His manhood qualifies. His Godhead gives Him power. He is a perfect Saviour. Look now upon the wood conjoined with gold, and see how the bright Tabernacle's wall reflects this Gospel of God's grace.

All skill was used to tighten and to brace the work. The corners were most carefully made fast. Five binding bars cemented the whole frame. Thus it was compact in solidity. This shows our Jesus as redemption's Samson. What arms of might are needed for His task! Hell's gates are strong: they must be borne away. Heaven's portals move not at a slender touch: they must be opened wide. The blows of Satan have terrific force: they must be all sustained. The weight of one least sin would crush a million worlds: all must be carried far from the sight of God. The cares and need of the redeemed are burdens of unmeasured mass. Beneath this load, before all shocks, Christ stands unshaken as these mystic walls. Reader, you may confide in Him. He cannot fall. Omnipotence cements His prowess.

The Tent was divided. There was a lower and a second room. Faith hence is taught that there are diverse grades in the knowledge of the Lord. They who see much may yet see more. They who dive deep may still go deeper. They who soar high find higher heights. My soul, let not your wings hang down. Let each moment be an onward flight. The vail will soon be passed, and heaven display full glories to your view.

The entrance-curtain hangs from five pillars. Four only hold the inner vail. The lessening number seems to teach that opening space expands to welcome the advancing saint. If any find the first gate to be strait, let them press on. Each progress leaves some hindrance behind. The end of holy conflict and unflinching faith is wide admission to the courts of heaven.

Lastly, the coverings have a voice. Spirit of Truth, speak by them to our hearts. The first has no inviting look. Its colour shines not. Its texture is uncouth. Thus to the worldling, Jesus shows no charms. The eye which seeks some tinsel-glitter will turn away in scorn. But there is folly and much peril here. Offence at the meek Saviour's lowly guise may be a rapid downfall into hell's worst depths.

But while faith gazes, the aspect changes. The second garb is red. The sign is not ambiguous. It testifies of blood. He who would save must die. From wounded sides and pierced hands a crimson stream must flow. This cries for pardon. This atones for guilt. This pays all debts. True Gospel-hope is a rich treasure from a blood-stained field. Pure Gospel-light shines from behind a blood-red cloud.

Beneath the red a snow-pure sheet appears. This sign, too, is a Bible-leaf. We read the spotless purity which shone in Christ. He bears man's flesh without one stain of sin. We see, too, the cleansing power of His blood. All washed therein are whiter than the snow-clad hills.

But look again. The tent now sparkles in variety of hues. The dazzling forms of shining cherubim adorn it. My soul, look onward to the day when Christ your Lord shall come. All faithful eyes shall see Him, fair in salvation's beauty, bright in salvation's glory, crowned with salvation's crown, praised with salvation's hymns. Reader, in that day will you shout and sing?

We cannot quit the Tent, and not observe the absence of a floor. Solemn the warning! Nothing which pictures Christ may lie beneath unheeding feet. No paschal blood was wasted on the threshold. No type of Christ is trodden down. Let the poor scoffer fear. The wages of contempt are paid in hell.

Another lesson craves our hearing. No door is closed. All day, all night, the Tabernacle stands open. No bolts, no bars obstruct. It seems to court approach. Such is the Saviour with His outstretched arms, calling poor sinners to His very heart. The lips of ever-willing love are ever open. Why will ye perish? Come to Me.

The Tent was a token of a present God. There He was pledged to commune with His sons: to show His face: to hear their cry: so in Christ Jesus heaven meets earth, and earth ascends to heaven. The Father comes and clasps the guilty to His arms. The guilty come and find a home in God. Eternal smiles chase fears away, and reconciliation claps her hands. The sinner asks, the Father gives. The Father gives, the sinner asks yet more. And more bestowed calls forth the louder praise. Here mercy sings, and grace exults, and happy concord reigns, and love waves high an olive-branch of peace.

Reader, leave not these humble lines until you find that Christ, the Tabernacle, makes you thus one with God for ever.

THE BRAZEN ALTAR

'Thou shalt make an Altar of shittim-wood, five cubits long and
five cubits broad; the Altar shall be four-square, and the height
thereof shall be three cubits. And thou shalt make the horns of it
upon the four corners thereof: his horns shall be of the same: and
thou shalt overlay it with brass.' Exod. 27.1, 2.

A spacious court enclosed the Tabernacle. There was admit-
tance by one only gate. All worshippers must pass one door.
Immediately in front of this the Brazen Altar stood. This
object first arrested view. Each eye must first behold, each
step must first approach its hallowed structure.

All heaven-taught souls acknowledge Jesus as the Altar
of the Church. Most plain instruction flows, then, from this
prominent position. Christ should be foremost in the heart's
desires. Each thought should first go forth towards Him.
He should receive the first-fruits of our love. His ear should
hear our earliest praise. He should be felt, the Alpha of life's
every move.

Parents and ministers mark this. In all your teaching
make Christ the morning-star. Let His sweet rays precede
all other light. Let other knowledge follow in His rear, and
be the lowly handmaid of pure wisdom's Lord.

The Brazen Altar faced the entrance-gate. It was a
solemn sight. Perpetual fire blazed. Perpetual smoke went
up. Perpetual victims died. Perpetual blood was shed. Perpetual offerings came.

Why must this carnage be? Who slew all these? What
kindled such devouring flames? These questions lead us to
an awful truth. Fire is the dreadful sign of wrath. The Altar
smokes, then, because wrath is gone forth – because transgressions must pay death. These flames write glaringly, See
what sin earns.

Reader, you cannot weigh enough the misery and guilt

f sin. It wakes eternal fury. It is the fuel of the quenchless
re. And what are you but one vile mass of sin? How, then,
an you escape? There is one only hope. This Altar shows
t. Come, now, and see its saving wonders. Come, seek its
efuge. Come, receive pardon from its blood-stained horns.
Pass by it – and you pass to bear, unsheltered, the thunder-
olts of wrath.

The Altar's component parts first bid us pause. Its two-
old substance presents the twofold nature of our Lord.
f frequent types show forth this truth, it is that frequent
houghts may cluster round it. If this sweet flower be frag-
ant in all spots of Scripture's field, it is that grateful hands
nay pluck it at each turn.

The frame is choicest wood combined with brass. The
vood alone could not suffice. The flames would quickly give
t, as ashes, to the sporting winds. A mass, too, of unmingled
rass would be a weight too cumbrous for a journeying
ost. The union fits the Altar for its destined use.

Here is our Jesus, the mighty God, the lowly man. As
od, He deals with God. As man, He takes the sinner's
lace. The God-man saves because the God-man suffers.
The pains sufficed for they are infinite. He touches heaven
nd earth and makes both one. The double substance aptly
ows how this rare suitableness combines in Christ.

The form is square. It stands the massive symbol of soli-
ity. It manifests the front which best resists all efforts to
bvert it. Faith sees this and exults in its stronghold. Christ
Salvation's Rock. The raging billows of hell's fury lash
Iim in vain. Earth's ceaseless hate can give no shock. He
ts in triumph on the shivered fragments of opposing arms.
he wit, the arguments, the sneers of man, have all fallen
armless at His feet. The cause of Christ still rears its con-
uering head. He reigns, and ever will reign, immovable
might.

123

Reader, this image calls us to deeper trust. Christ's truth, Christ's word, Christ's work, can never be cast down.

This shape presents to every quarter the same front. B the approach from east, from west, from north, from south the aspect changes not. Thus Jesus meets the sinner's eye, in every age, in every place, the same. There is no averted look There is no half reception. There is one broad display o manifested and inviting grace. Sinner, four equal sides fac every point. They meet you at each turn. Expanded arm bid you draw near.

Horns branch, too, from each quarter. These are a well known sign. They speak of all-subduing might. The horned tribes move as the forest's terror. When they assail, the triumph. Christ is thus armed for conquest. The thought i precious. My soul, revolve it oft. Self is a broken arm, a pointless dart, a crumbling staff. But strong assaults mus be repelled, and strong corruptions trodden down, and strong temptations baffled, and heavy trials borne. Man' sinews cannot wrestle with such foes. But Christ is near. Re ceive Him as your sword of strength. Leaning on Him poor worms thresh mountains, and earth's feeblest thing do valiantly. Hence the grand power of that wondrou word, 'I can do all things through Christ that strengtheneth me.' It is the horn of Jesus, which prevails. It never can b broken. Therefore His people raise the head: and victor is their crown.

These horns were more than types of strength. They wer realities of refuge. The criminals who touch must live. Th sword of vengeance lost its power here. All peril died. Th spot was hallowed safety. This is the full security of Christ' protecting arms. Satan can no more harm. Can He seiz Christ, and drag Him from His throne? He must do thi ere he can pluck the weakest sinner from the breast o Christ. O my soul, let nothing part you from salvation' horns. Let all your guilt, let every view of sin, let the drea thunder of the threatening law, let the swift darts of wrath quicken your flight to Him. Adhere to Him. Hold fast by Him. Live in His wounds. There is no other spot of peace.

The Altar's main design was to receive burnt-offerings. At early morn, throughout the day, at evening's close, the flames were bright, the spire of smoke ascended. He has no Gospel-light who sees not Christ in all this blaze. Each fire-made offering typified His death.

But on what Altar can Christ place Himself? The promised God-man comes to die: what arms are able to bear Him up? All things below are worse than worthless for such glorious use. If structure could be reared, in which each stone were brighter than a million suns, it would be black beside Him. Creation has no fit support. When Jehovah's fellow dies, Jehovah's fellow must sustain Himself.

Men little think what burdens pressed Him down. The least transgression of God's righteous law is load beyond all thought. Its weight would sink the sinner deeper and deeper through unending ages in unfathomable gulfs. But this holy victim bears the countless sins of countless multitudes. What can support Him when the avenging fire falls? Angels have no sufficient arms. The help of worlds would crumble into dust. Earth can supply no prop or pillar. Christ alone can now uphold Himself. His Deity alone can keep humanity uncrushed. Christ's only Altar is Himself.

Reader, pause now. Behold God's Altar and God's Offering. Christ stands, the fire-applying Priest. Christ comes, the fire-receiving Lamb. Christ lies, the fire-sustaining Altar. All is sufficient, for all is divine. There is enough in all, for there is God in all.

The wrath breaks forth. The fury is outpoured. Vengeance demands her due. The Law exacts its curse. But the burnt-offering fails not. Each attribute of God exults. Each sin of the whole family is expiated. Christ bears the whole, because an Altar, strong as His Godhead, bears Him to the end.

There is no sweeter thought on earth, there is no louder song in heaven, than praise to the Priest who offered, to the Lamb which suffered, to the Altar which sustained.

Reader, survey again salvation's fabric in its wondrous parts. Extend your hand. Write glory on each stone. It is all worthy of Him who willed, of Him who planned, of Him who wrought it out. God comes. God comes in flesh to die. God upholds the victim in His dying. Christ is the gift, the Altar, the All.

My soul, here is a remedy for all your sins. Your need is great, but the atonement is far greater.

Reader, this Altar still stands high in heaven. It stands, and sinners may draw near and use it. Heed, then, a solemn word. Do you discern it with faith's clear eye? Do you cling to it with faith's strong hand? Do you prize it, as God's best gift? Do you frequent it, as your soul's loved home? Is life's main work transacted here?

Need, urgent need there is, that hearts should be thus probed. Time is, at most, but very short, and rapid is its ceaseless flight. Eternity with all its magnitudes is at the door. The last breath may be quivering on the lip. Undying souls are on the threshold of eternal doom. And Satan strives, with every art, to close our eyes and lure us to his nets. The world surrounds us with its poisoned-baits. It checks us with its sneers and frowns. It courts us with its treacherous smiles. Self, too, is no soul-friend. It acts a traitor's part. It opens to the murderous foe. Hence there is need that honest lips should press home honest truth. Say, then, is Christ the precious Altar of your faith, your joy, your hope, your love, your zeal? Look inward. Search yourself. In every age, not least in this, Satan erects his many counterfeits, and calls them Christ. He decks them with false show. He slopes a flowery path to the bewitching snare.

He smooths with skilful hand the slippery descent. He plants the altar of man's fancied worth. He prompts the dream, that rubbish dug from nature's quarry, and shaped by sin-soiled hands, and worked by sin-soiled tools, may form a sufficient base. He bids men offer Christ on this, and then lie down content.

Reader, cast such coiled vipers from your breast. What! pile sin on sin, add filth to filth, and call it a fit pedestal for Christ! The very thought is hell's worst lie. No! Christ must be all, or nothing. He must do all the work, have all the merit, and bear all the glory. Would that they whose hearts turn fondly towards Rome's frauds, would hear. They often sound the Altar's name – but they tread down the Altar's truth. They build, indeed, a Babel-tower. They raise high steps, as an ascent to heaven. But is Christ there, the First, the Last, the All? Far otherwise. Man's merit lays the broad foundation. His tears of self-wrought penitence, his long array of self-denials, his train of vaunted charities, his studied postures, and his outside rites, construct the fabric. Such is their altar. Christ then, in name, is added, as a fair jewel to an earth-made crown. Thus proud conceit and Satan's fraud join hand in hand to cast down Christ.

Reader, such altars stand on ruin's ground. They decorate a downward path. Think what the end must be of Christ-denying creeds, and Christ-rejecting worship, and Christ-ignoring forms?

Are you this dreamer? Awake! Awake! Hell has its altar, too. On it lost souls lie down for ever. Satan's bellows will not cease to blow. Tormenting anguish will not cease to flare. But imperishable victims cannot be consumed. Awake! Awake! Behold! heaven's saving Altar is not yet beyond your reach.

THE PRIEST

'Take thou unto thee Aaron thy brother, and his sons with him, from among the children of Israel, that he may minister unto Me, in the Priest's office.' Exod. 28.1

No pencil's art can represent the sun. No marble can express the eye. No image can portray Christ's riches. He leaves all boundaries behind. But still His knowledge is the soul's choice food. It is the joy of joys, it is the life of life.

The tabernacle stood to be the witness of His truth. The Altar was upraised, the victims died, the incense curled, the lamps were lighted, the shew-bread was presented, to paint in varied ways His varied worth.

These many types taught much. But this full cluster is not a full picture. A living office, therefore, receives birth. An active order is now added. The Priest appears, to be an ever-moving semblance of redeeming work.

Reader, we live in times when erring lips mis-personate our Lord. But err we cannot, when we behold Him in the Priestly ordinance.

Our Priest is not on earth. The Spirit witnesses, 'We have a great High-priest, that is passed into the heavens.' Heb. 4.14. Who can this be but Christ? Thus Christ is the Priest who ministers for us. Ignorance makes many priests. Faith knows but one.

First, mark the call. It is most clear. No human mind selects the Priest. No self-called man usurps the work. The service is ordained by God. The sacred order has a door which none can pass but by divine command. The heavenly will thus speaks: 'Take thou unto thee Aaron thy brother, and his sons with him.' The purport is distinct; 'No man taketh this honour unto himself, but he that is called of God, as was Aaron.' Heb. 5.4. In Christ the fulfilment is found. 'So also Christ glorified not Himself to be made an

High-Priest; but He that said unto Him, Thou art my Son, to-day have I begotten Thee.' Heb. 5.5

There is a volume of instruction here. Christ swiftly flies on outstretched wings of love. But all the flight, and all the course are in the path which God marked out. The Father chooses and the Father sends. The Son obeys and hastens to the work. Hence all poor sinners may repose, without one fear, on Christ. He comes commissioned to discharge a settled service. He saves according to decree.

The office is protected by another fence. None can pass through who have defect. The interdict is stern. All who draw near must show completeness in complete perfection. Thus saith the Lord, 'Whosoever he be of thy seed in their generations that hath any blemish, let him not approach to offer the bread of his God.' Lev. 21.17. This leads us to explore the all-surpassing worthiness of Christ. He is beauty in its full-blown blaze, and grace in its most graceful form. He is as bright as God is bright. He is as perfect as God is perfect. Righteousness is His girdle. Glory is His robe. The very heavens are unclean beside Him.

Reader, keep Jesus always in your sight. The world in all its tinsel-show will then no more be seen. This admiration has transforming power. Faith looks, and as it looks, an inward likeness grows. We 'are changed into the same image from glory to glory, even as by the Spirit of the Lord.' 2 Cor. 3.18. He is the holiest man who sees by faith the most of Christ.

Let Christ, then, take the Priesthood for His people. He has full worthiness. No sin ever stained Him.

Through this vestibule, we may press on to view the Priestly work itself. It is a tree of many branches. The main are thus described: 'Every High-priest taken from among men is ordained for men in things pertaining to God, that he may offer both gifts and sacrifices for sins.' Heb. 5.1. At the altar the chief functions were discharged. There is an altar, then, at which Jesus served. Calvary shows it. Let faith, with open and adoring eye, survey that scene. It gladdens heaven and affrights all hell. It should be meditation's happiest seat. The promised Lamb appears. The victim chosen before time began, the theme of prophet's song, the crown of patriarchal hope, the jewel in each typifying casket, is now led forth. It is the God-man Jesus, Jehovah's fellow, creation's author, the Lord of all things, the Prince of life. He comes to die, that He may save; to bleed, that He may make atonement; to lay down life, that sin may be destroyed. An altar is prepared. It is sufficient for the mighty load. Its pillars are the strength of Deity.

But what Priest leads this Lamb and binds Him to the Altar? The Priest is Jesus. He teaches this when speaking of His life. He says, 'No man taketh it from Me, but I lay it down of Myself.' John 10.18. The Spirit bids us mark the Sacrificer's hand, when He adds, He 'through the eternal Spirit, offered Himself without spot to God.' Heb. 9.14. Jesus well knew that nothing but His blood could satisfy, and He did not withhold it. He loved to save, and therefore loved to die. He joyed to do His Father's will, and therefore joyed to give Himself. The language of the cross is loud and clear. All that my Father's glory asks – all that My people's need requires – I willingly present. I gladly die to honour God and bring redemption to My flock.

My soul, turn often to the self-sacrificing act. Do you seek proof that He desires your pardon? Behold it in His arm stretched out to give Himself. You must be spared. He will not spare Himself.

But when the blood was shed, the Priestly work was not concluded. On the most solemn day of Israel's year, the High-priest passed the vail. He stood before the mercy-seat. But not without the proof of sacrifice enacted. He brought the blood. He sprinkled it before the ark.

Is Jesus here? What is the Spirit's comment. 'By His

own blood, He entered in once into the holy place, having obtained eternal redemption for us.' Heb. 9.12.

We thus gain vision of the courts above. Our eyes are opened to a wondrous sight. We see our Jesus transacting still the priestly functions.

My soul, be much in spirit, and by faith, in heaven. It is a sin, a shame, a folly, and a loss, to live apart from Him who ever lives for you. Abide by Jesus. He is never absent from the Father's side. He ever shows His soul-redeeming blood. It has an eloquence which must prevail. It has a plea which no accusing rage can answer. It is full price for all the ransomed race. It fills the scales which justice brings. It gives to truth its every demand. It silences the Law's stern curse. It claims all pardon, and all sins are pardoned. What now can Satan say? The High-priest shows the blood. All charge is answered, all guilt removed, the blood-bought are absolved.

The High-priest bears a censer, too. From it a cloud of rising incense covers all the mercy-seat. Lev. 16.12, 13. Thus Jesus fills the heavens with fragrance. His precious intercession sheds precious odours round. He pleads that all His work on earth is done. He spreads His wounded hands. He shows His wounded side. He proves that every term of the vast covenant of grace is kept, that sin is punished, and His people free. Oh! the rich savour of such rich pleas! All attributes take up the shout, 'Who shall lay anything to the charge of God's elect?'

The High-priest exercised another function. It was his happy province to strew blessings round. 'Speak unto Aaron and unto His sons, saying, On this wise ye shall bless the children of Israel.' Num. 6.23. Jesus is called to be a blessing Lord. Mark His departing act: 'He led them out as far as to Bethany, and He lifted up His hands and blessed them.' Luke 24.50. And now He lives in heaven a blessing-life, and opens there His blessing-hands, and utters there His blessing-voice, and displays there His blessing-smile.

Poor sinners feel their sin. They see the Saviour. They flee to wash in His all-cleansing blood. They hide beneath His glorious righteousness. This is a blessing. They burst the bonds of sin and Satan; they love the sacred feasts of Bible-truth and holy ordinances; they glory in the sealing sacraments. This is a blessing. They rejoice with joy unspeakable; they trample on the world, and all its snares, and all its baits. They see hell vanquished, heaven their home, saints their brethren, angels their ministering guardians, Jesus their all. This is a blessing. Life is theirs; Death is theirs; Christ is theirs; Heaven is theirs; Glory is theirs; Eternity is theirs. This is a blessing. All these streams flow down from Jesus our High-priest, who ever lives to execute this blessing work.

It is the Spirit's earnest will that we should know and use this Great High-priest. Hence, by repeated contrasts, He magnifies His worth. This teaching bids us give ear. Let us advance, then, and pluck some fruit from these luxuriant boughs.

Read Heb. 7.23. The priests who ministered to Israel's sons were only men. Dust was their substance and to dust they soon returned. Death soon removed them from their post. Our Great High-priest is very God. His life is immortality. Eternity is His day. No time can bring decay to Him. No age makes His seat void. So long as mediating work remains, His mediating office lives.

Read Heb. 7.27. They were corruption's seed. Sin cleaved to their most holy service. Their very best was vile and black. They must make offerings for themselves. They needed blood to wash away their guilt. Jesus is pure as God is pure. He breathed no atmosphere but perfect holiness. Poor sinners have a sinless Priest in Him.

Read Heb. 9.7. They passed the vail but once in every

year. He entered heaven as His own abode. There, day and night He pleads, and will present incessant pleas, until the latest saint be safely gathered home.

Read Heb. 9.12. Their victims were but creatures of this lower world. The blood was only blood of beasts. It had no saving power. It could not touch trangression's infinite pollution. Jesus presents Himself to God. He brings the very blood of God. All worlds are worthless when compared to this. Believer, this is your full salvation.

Read Heb. 10.11. They offered often. The victims died, the altars blazed, the incense burned from year to year, from day to day. Jesus presents one victim once. His death once died, His life once given, His blood once shed, fully and for ever washed out His people's sins, redeemed His people's lives, and saved His people's souls. His one surrender of Himself as the atoning Lamb, for ever quenched all wrath, for ever took away all curse, for ever satisfied all claims, for ever saved the family of faith, for ever opened heaven, for ever vanquished hell. To add to infinite perfection is impossible. Woe be to them who think such offering incomplete!

The Spirit cries, 'Consider the Apostle and High-priest of our profession, Christ Jesus.' Heb. 3.1. Reader, obey. Make Him the centre of your every thought, the home of your adoring mind, the first, the last of meditation's joys. Christ's Priesthood is a theme which time cannot exhaust. It is a theme for which eternity is short.

THE HOLY GARMENTS

'Thou shalt make Holy Garments for Aaron thy brother, for glory and for beauty.' Exod. 28.2

If ever eyes beheld an object in which splendour shone, it was the high-priest in his Holy Garments. God planned each part 'for glory and for beauty.' Hence every brilliant colour sparkled. Hence richest jewels cast back dazzling rays. The rainbow's varied hues, the sun's meridian light, seemed to concentrate in a human form. Earth brought her best. Art framed them with a Spirit-given skill.

Reader, such is the figure to which these humble pages would now invite your gaze. But you will look in vain if you see nothing but the costly robes. Here is delight for faith's enraptured heart. Jesus is here. What is beauty, but His form, His grace, His work! What is glory, but His manifested sight! This workmanship would never have seen birth, except to show His all-surpassing worth.

Spirit of Truth look down! We long for clearer vision of the Lord. It is Thy sovereign province to display Him. Cause, then, these Holy Garments to fulfil their office.

First, there was the inmost coat. Its texture was of finest linen. Exod. 28.39. It covered the whole frame. It clothed the arms and flowed down to the ground. It thus showed purity from head to foot.

Do any ask: Where can such full-length purity be found? The Gospel answers by revealing Christ. He is one blaze of spotless righteousness. This truth is the firm pedestal of all our hopes. If one defect had touched Him, He must have brought antonement for Himself. But being sinless, He can take the sinner's place. He hangs a sinless body on the cross. He gives a sinless soul to bear God's wrath. Thus wrath is satisfied.

The snow-white vest exhibits, too, the righteousness which Christ wrought out on earth. His active obedience covers the whole surface of the law. Heaven's palace must have heaven-pure garments. Christ weaves them. Christ bestows them. Faith takes them, and is thus made fit for the throne of God.

Reader, think well; you must sink low in hell, except a righteous Saviour cleanse your guilt. You cannot stand before God's eye, except you face Him righteous as He is righteous. You cannot breathe in heaven, except a new-born nature love its holy clime. The hands of Jesus hold all this mercy for you. His holy blood is perfect expiation. His full obedience is your royal robe. His Spirit can impart all grace. Behold the High-priest in this inner vest, and let its snow-white hue teach you these truths.

The coat was tightly fastened by a girdle. To gird the loins was to prepare for toil. Activity is thus insured. This sign, then, shows our Jesus equipped for all the labours of redeeming service. It was no light task to save souls. Mountains of difficulty must be overcome. Untiring strength must be put forth. He promptly strains each energy. He meets each foe. He clears each obstacle. He rests not till the path from earth to heaven is free. Yet He will work until His flock is safely gathered home. He worked on earth because He greatly loved. He works in heaven because He loves as greatly.

Reader, see Jesus all activity to save. He never flags nor loiters nor desists. One thing He does. He girds His loins for labour. Are you as earnest to be saved? Are you as active to seek Him? Are you as zealous to subserve His cause? His persevering zeal should shame man's listless indolence. His girdle is reproach to our ungirded loins.

Above the coat a robe was placed. Exod. 28.31. In measure it was less. It had no covering for the arms. It scarcely reached below the knees. But its chief difference was its

135

lovely hue, and the magnificence of the bordering hem. The colour was pure blue. It thus reflected the clear canopy of heaven. The high-priest ministered in a sky-blue robe. Thus Jesus brings all heaven to our thought. Heaven is in His every word. His hands extend the gift of heaven. To see Him now is heaven begun. To be with Him for ever is heaven complete. Faith knows no heaven but Him.

Reader, see Jesus as your High-priest in azure robe, and you will die to earth, and earth will die to you. A brighter scene will win you to love brighter things.

This robe had a rich fringe. Its hem was a broad belt of pomegranates and golden bells. These pomegranates were richly worked in purple, blue, and scarlet. Of all the fruits, this is most rich in seed. Therefore it is fit emblem of luxuriant shoots. Here Jesus is portrayed, as the 'Everlasting Father' of a countless race. His blood is sown on earth; a harvest of saved souls springs up. Mark the crowds who throng the throne of glory. They all are produce of redeeming love. Mark all who in the wilderness of earth show signs of new-imparted being. They all derive existence from one stem; they all are fruit of one regenerating Spirit. We see the ornamented edge, and we adore the truth, 'So shall thy seed be.' Gen. 15.5.

The pomegranates were intermingled with golden bells. The high-priest could not stir but melody announced that he was near. Israel's sons found special comfort in this ordinance. Their high-priest passed the vail. He stood before the ark. It was a solemn moment. The spot was terrible in awe. The thought might rise, Can man draw near to symbols of God's glory and not die? But a sweet note lulls all such fears to rest. The golden bells are heard. All hearts rejoiced. The high-priest faced the mercy-seat and yet he lived. The golden bells still sound. Faith is no stranger to their voice. Jesus, indeed, is no more seen by mortal sense. The heavens hide Him. He prosecutes His work before an unseen throne.

And there He lives. The proof is clear and sweet as music from the golden bells. Each tender whisper of His love, each soothing application of His word, each sweet assurance of unfailing care, are sounds which evidence that Jesus lives. The golden bells for ever ring the joyful tidings, 'Because I live, ye shall live also.'

Believer, look often to the fringe of the blue robe. Jesus is there, the fruitful author of your every grace. Jesus is there, assuring that He lives to give you life.

The ephod was next added. Exod. 28.6. This was a tunic, shorter in form than the preceding robe. But while the robe was simple in one azure shade, this was all radiant in diversity of hue. They shall make it, said the Lord, 'of gold, of blue, of purple, of scarlet, and fine twined linen, with cunning work.' Each brought its choicest produce. Art used its utmost effort. The purport is most clear. We thus are taught that all rare graces are combined in Christ. His person, which is God and man; His work, which fills all heaven with glory; His tender dealings; His loving heart; His faithful truth; these are the perfection of all charms. None ever see true beauty till Christ appears in His salvation's robes.

Two shoulder-pieces fixed it. No common skill prepared them. Sockets of gold were formed. In each an onyx stone was placed. These stones were graven with the names of Israel's tribes.

O my soul, what streams of comfort issue from this sight! Your name, your very name appears on high, uplifted on the shoulders of your Lord. How then can foes work harm? They may assail, they will assail. But you are high above their reach. Can they scale heaven? The thought is folly. Yet they must lay Christ low before they can touch you. Your seat is safety. Your prop is Deity. Rejoice, be glad. High is your Lord – are you less high? Thus, weak in yourself, you soar above all peril, and sit as more than conqueror on eminence of Almightiness.

Rich is this comfort. But the Lord of comfort yet gives more. It is His will that joy unspeakable should fill His people's souls. A breast-plate therefore is inserted in this ephod's front. No words can show its matchless slendour. Upon a ground richly embroidered like the ephod, twelve precious jewels were set. Each glittering stone exhibited the name of one of Israel's tribes.

This work is all arranged to prove how dearly Jesus loves His own. The world may scorn them as the vilest dust. But Jesus guards them as His choicest treasure, and put them on as the delight of His delights. Redeemed souls are His chief ornament. He wears them on His heart.

Believer, look to Christ. Mark, He displays His very heart. What read you there? Your name! Your very name! Do you ask, And can He love me? Surely the manger, the garden, and the cross are proof. But lest such evidence should not suffice, His front is shown as a scroll written with your name. Be then persuaded. His life is love for you. His heart has never been, and never will be, without your image. You dwell entwined amid affection's fibres. Your High-priest ever wears this precious breast-plate. He ever shows your name before God's throne. You are inseparable portion of His breast.

This is not all. The breast-plate holds more wondrous treasure yet. But here is mystery which we cannot scan. We know, and it is much to know, that the Urim and Thummin were adjoined. The meaning of the terms is clear. Their voice is 'light and perfection.' Their holy use is also known. By means of these the Lord revealed His will, and gave responses to the consulting priest. The Gospel of the ordinance is likewise clear. Christ is our light. He is our full perfection. Do we need wisdom? Do we seek guidance? We may draw near. From His heart pure light will shine. Do we mourn that imperfection cleaves as our very skin? He only can relieve. His blood, His righteousness, His Spirit, His dealings, are perfect and make perfect.

Reader, seek Christ, and light is yours. Seek Christ, and all perfection is your portion. Our Urim and our Thummin are His smile.

The Holy Garments are not yet complete. The head must now receive its crowning grace. For this a mitre is prepared. Fair linen is the substance. A belt of blue surrounds it. On this a golden plate is fixed. And then the glorious name, 'HOLINESS TO THE LORD,' shines forth. Exod. 28.36. My soul, look up to heaven. Jesus there ministers to consummate salvation. What is it that His front declares? 'HOLINESS TO THE LORD.' Adore Him: for such is His just title. His person is 'HOLINESS TO THE LORD.' Unspotted purity is His essence. If it were otherwise, He could not take a Saviour's place. His work is 'HOLINESS TO THE LORD.' He came to sanctify Himself, that He might do His Father's will. His blood, His righteousness, His prayers, are 'HOLINESS TO THE LORD.' His people, in their souls, their walk, their ways, are 'HOLINESS TO THE LORD.' He found them sinners. He made them holy. He gave them new hearts, new lives, to be for ever 'HOLINESS TO THE LORD.'

Such is our robed High-priest. Is He not glory? Is He not beauty? Who will not love Him? Who will not praise Him? Who will not pray, Glorify me in Thy glory – Beautify me in Thy beauty – for I am Thine?

THE GOLDEN ALTAR

'Thou shalt make an Altar to burn incense upon.' Exod. 30.1

He whose daily life is an upward flight to Christ has heaven on his way to heaven. Wide indeed are these fields of light. We may journey far, but they stretch farther. From every point more lofty heights appear. The subject is a book whose pages end not. The more it occupies us, the less it wearies. It richly feeds, but ever leaves an appetite for more.

The Redeemer's image is embodied in the Tabernacle-service. 'Behold Him, behold Him,' is the one universal cry. But nowhere is this voice more plainly heard than at the Golden Altar. This filled the tent with richest streams of fragrance. So it preached Him who is the Incense of the courts above.

Reader, this now invites our notice. In mercy may the Spirit cause the sacred odour to arise.

The station of this Altar first claims thought. The Lord, who orders all things with wise end, especially enjoins, 'Thou shalt put it before the vail that is by the ark of the testimony.' Exod. 30.6. Mark where he stands, then, who discharges service at this shrine. The expiating altar is behind. His steps have brought him to the borders of the holiest place. He has passed the spot where dying victims bleed. Heaven's clearest emblem is now close. Thus the Altar's chosen position seems as a link to join the cross and crown.

Reader, the spot calls you to pause and look within. Say, have your feet attained this station? Has the first altar seen you humble, guilt-stricken, smiting on your breast, and confessing all your miserable sins before it? Has eager faith there touched the atoning Lamb? Is pardon in your hand?

Is your soul calm in knowledge of the curse removed and full remission given? Have you thus pressed towards this inner Altar, where the incense burns? If so, the vail is almost touched. This screens the sanctuary, which pictures heaven's bright rest. The space is narrow now, which parts you from eternal bliss. The ever-smiling smile of God, the ever-present presence of the Lamb is your near portion. Swift-flying moments will soon waft you to the kingdom from all eternity prepared, through all eternity prolonged.

Reader, is such in very truth your place? If so, adore the grace which led you to it. You may have wealth. It cannot profit long. You may have health. Decay will cause its flower to fade. You may have strength. It soon will totter to the grave. You may have honours. A breath will blast them. You may have flattering friends. They are but as a summer brook. These boasted joys oft cover now an aching heart. They never gave a grain of solid peace. They never healed a conscience-wound. They never won approving looks from heaven. They never crushed the sting of sin.

But floods of peace surround this golden shrine. Its worshippers hold mercy and eye glory. They look back on all transgression blotted out. Heaven's rays are breaking on their blood-washed souls. The second Altar is so set that these truths sparkle from its instant sight.

Next, let this Altar's parts be viewed. No human mind designs. God, who gives Christ, gives each foreshadowing sign. His voice directs, 'Let gold be joined to wood.' Christ is the corresponding wonder. He is equal to God in Godhead's greatness, and fellow to man in humanity's low state. He is bold to ascend to Jehovah's throne, and willing to share the sinner's rags.

Such is the Saviour whom God sends. Such is the Saviour whom sin needs. More cannot be. Less would be nothing worth. Would that all tribes of men could form one audience, to hear one word from these poor lips. It should be this: A God-man only can redeem a sinner's soul. A God-man, even Jesus, undertakes the work. A God-man, even Jesus, finishes the whole.

Its form is square. Such is the shape, too, of the atoning altar. We thus are taught again, that our salvation is exceeding strong. It is support which cannot fail. It is most firmly based on God's own might for ever.

We further learn that one inviting front is turned to every comer. From every quarter, then, let sinners flee hither. Christ never did, He never will, He never can reject. One face, arrayed in ready welcomes, smiles on all.

It had its crown, its horns, its staves. Each sounds glad tidings to faith's listening ear.

The crown is royal emblem. Let Jesus take it, then. It is His right. The prophet sings, 'The government shall be upon His shoulder.' Is. 9.6. The Father cries, 'Yet have I set my King upon My holy hill of Zion.' Ps. 2.6. Once, indeed, derision mocked Him with its circling thorns. But now in heaven He wears redemption's everlasting diadem.

But though He rules thus high, His darling throne is the poor sinner's heart. His brightest crown is jewelled with saved souls.

The horns speak mighty prowess. They prove that victory is on His brow. It is so. No strength can stand before Christ's front. He speaks and He prevails. Hell quakes. The captives come forth free. Sin's chain is shivered. Opposing lusts lie down subdued. The baffled world is trodden under foot.

Believer, at this Altar, then, cast out all fear. A conquered kingdom cannot conquer you. A horn has pierced each adversary's heart. You stride to triumphs over death-stricken ranks.

The staves were signs of readiness to move. The Gospel-sound must go into all the earth. Place has no power to shut out Christ. He penetrates the lonely wastes. He cheers

Elijah by the desert brook. No bars give hindrance. He wakes a song within Paul's inmost cell. He watches by the wandering Jacob. He walks beside the faithful youths in the furnace-heat. He animates the warring Joshua. He stoops to poverty's most squalid mire, and sits beside the outcast Lazarus. He mounts the steps of lofty palaces, and guards His followers in Caesar's household. There is no pilgrim in the fleet, the camp, the rustic hut, the lordly fort, the hall of science, whose heart Christ cannot reach. His swiftly-flying love calls all His children in from east, from west, from north, from south. They all draw near to Him because He first draws near to them.

Believer, at this altar learn that in life's busiest haunts, in retreat's solitary hours, Christ is an attending friend.

It is true that here no victim died. But is it true, that here no blood was seen? Oh! no. On solemn days, which saw atoning rites so solemnly performed, blood was here largely scattered. The high-priest dyed these horns, and sprinkled this holy vessel seven times.

Reader, be wise, and learn the heaven-taught art of mixing blood with every service. Let prayer be mighty in the plea of Jesu's death. Let praise ascend from blood-cleansed lips. Let love be as a flame from blood-besprinkled hearts. Let every work be worked with blood-washed hands. God's eye looks for this sign. When it is seen, mercy's wide door flies open, and acceptance cannot delay. But woe is theirs whose offerings are not so washed. Cain's miserable end gives warning that we bring no sacrifice without atonement.

But this Altar's main use was to receive the incense. Here the sacred spice was burned. When the morning lamps were trimmed, and when the evening lights were lit, the perfumed flame was kindled.

Reader, observe the process. The fire was first brought. The holy powder was then spread. The streams of odour then

143

flew high. And the whole tent was fragrant as the garden of the Lord.

The Spirit has selected incense as the type of prayer. 'Let my prayer be set forth before Thee as incense.' Ps. 141.2 We here, then, have a graphic image of the prayer of prayers, the intercession of the King-priest Jesus.

Mark whence the kindling fire was brought. It came not from a human hearth. The outer altar gave the supply. It was the very fire from heaven. It was the very fire which consumed each offering. Great truth is here involved. The victim-altar feeds the Incense-altar. The prayer of Christ receives its life, its power, its vigour, from His blood-stained cross. The argument which prevails is drawn from justice satisfied, from payment made, from wrath appeased, from law fulfilled, from curse endured, from covenant discharged. Christ's intercession rests upon His death.

Thus incense never ceases to ascend. Heaven is ever fragrant with its precious savour.

Compare all other knowledge with this truth. It flees and vanishes as an unsubstantial mist. This is the brightest jewel in the crown of grace. This is the fullest cordial in the Gospel-cup. Where is there joy like realizing views of the great work, which Christ now acts on high? He pleads. He lives to plead. He ever lives to plead. He shows His finished work. He stretches forth His pierced hands. He claims fulfilment of redemption's contract. Our heavenly Father joys in the grateful streams. His every attribute has infinite delight. He smiles approval. His ready hands are opened. All blessings are poured out. Pardons are sealed. The Spirit is bestowed. Ministering angels hasten to their guardian-work. The happy flock are gathered into the one fold of grace, and prepared for the one fold of glory.

O my soul, may this sweet incense be your constant joy! Shall heaven be glad, and you not clap the hand, and shout all praise? Learn more and more your high and privileged estate. Grasping these horns, you may cast back all doubts and fears which Satan would suggest. He oft will whisper that our prayers are weak and worthless, and nought but insults to the ears of God. Alas! this is too often true. But hope relies not on our holiest work. Christ prays. Christ prays most worthily. And in His prayers acceptance stands. Our praises are oft as a dull smouldering smoke. Alas! here is our sin, our shame, our base ingratitude. But Jesu's voice is heard. His merits sweeten our short-coming utterance. Our hearts are cold and dead. But Christ ever loves, and proves His love by unremitted prayers.

O my soul, think how prevailingly Christ works for you. Shall the king say to Esther, 'What is thy request? it shall be even given thee to the half of the kingdom.' Esther 5.3. And can the cry of God's co-equal Son be coldly met? Is the promise pledged, 'Whatsoever ye shall ask of the Father in My name, He will give it you?' John 16.23. And shall there be less acceptance when Christ in His own person supplicates? This cannot be. Prize, then, your Incense Altar. Delight in it. Use it until you pass the vail.

But hark! A word of solemn warning sounds. The incense is most hallowed. God adds, 'Whosoever shall make like unto that, to smell thereto, shall even be cut off from his people.' Exod. 30.38. The type profaned was hopeless death. Will any trifle with the grand reality? If common use were sacrilege, what must the rejection be?

Some join with it the fancied prayers of mediating saints. What! is there not enough in Christ? Can He be under-valued, and God pleased? Can they reach glory who rob Him of His crown?

THE LAVER

'Thou shalt also make a Laver of brass.' Exod. 30.18

Reader, whatever your earthly lot may be, your outward frame contains a priceless gem. You hold within you an immortal soul. Life's day admits variety of shade. But every state is a sure passage to a changeless home. Our common portion is eternity.

What, then, is man's grand concern? Surely, to make safe provision for this wondrous soul. What should be the first, the last of all his efforts? Surely to win endless happiness for endless days. This point is clear. All who can think, admit it.

God's Word directs us to life's only way. Oh! that His Spirit might give eyes to see it. The soul, by nature and by work, is one vile mass of sin. Christ only can remove these stains. The everlasting hope is lost through sad transgression. Christ only can restore it.

Hence, God from His high throne, Jesus in countless ways of love, the Spirit by most gracious strivings, the Bible in its every page, call sinners to accept the one great cure. Such is the aim which now knocks at your heart's door. Such motive brings the holy Laver to your sight. It is a clear-toned witness of redeeming grace. It paints in vivid rays the cleansing worth of Christ. Use it, and your soul is clean. Use it, and your eternity is joy.

God bids His servant to construct the Laver. 'Thou shalt also make a Laver of brass, and his foot also of brass, to wash withal: and thou shalt put it between the tabernacle of the congregation and the altar, and thou shalt put water therein.' Exod. 30.18.

Observe the choice material. It is brass. This strongest metal shadows forth the strength of Christ. He came to do

146

the mightiest of mighty works. And He brings omnipotence in His hand. But whence is the brass obtained? Whose hands supply it? The piety of females furnishes it. They gladly give their mirrors for this holy use. Exod. 38.8.

Faith seeks, nor seeks in vain, to gain instruction from this fact. Women give aid to form this Gospel-type. Here seems to be a bud of truth. The virgin-mother holds the full-blown flower. Look to Bethlehem's inn. There the meek Jesus lies, made of a woman, the kinsman of our race. The gift of gifts comes in through female means.

They bring their mirrors. The bias of their hearts is changed. New feelings bear new fruit. These recently were prized as implements of vanity, and handmaids of self-love. But now the eyes are opened to far nobler views. Self has no charms, when once the wondering gaze has caught some glimpse of things divine.

Reader, if your faith sees the glorious beauties of the Lord, surely all other features are a dismal blank.

The offering is not scorned. That which was framed to cast back poor nature's image is accepted to form semblances of grace. We see to what high use our worldly vanities may rise.

Reader, you perhaps have stores of needless show. Turn them to real benefits. Devote them to the Lord. Present them as the means to spread abroad some tidings of His truth. Forget not that the Laver, which in these pages preaches Christ, was brass from women's mirrors.

It occupied a midway space between the brazen altar and the tabernacle's door. A strict command was issued that no priest should touch the one or pass the other until his hands and feet had been here washed. Such is the ordinance. It sternly warns that no defilement may approach the Lord. It sweetly adds that He who demands such purity provides the purifying stream. The Lord who says that you must be cleansed, brings near His cleansing Laver.

Believer, mark well your calling. It is to minister a live-long service to the Lord. Life is not life, until each act sub-serves our God. Our feet should only move for Him. Our hands should know no work but His. But ah! these feet, these hands, how soiled, how black they are! The dust of earth forms a polluting path, and through it is our daily walk. The things of earth leave a defiling stain, and such we always handle. With feet, with hands like these, can we bring the sacrifice of faith, or burn the incense of devoted love?

But a Laver is prepared. It stands beside us at each step. It has a voice loud as the roar of many waves, sweet as the melody of heaven – Wash and be clean.

Eternal love devised the plan. Eternal wisdom drew the model. Eternal grace comes down to build it. But by whom can it be filled? Jesus Himself pours in the stream. He brings the rich supply. It is blood, blood from His own veins, blood from His very heart. Nothing in heaven or earth could help, but this. He bleeds, to fill the Laver. He dies, to open wide the pardoning fount.

But is there virtue in this flood to wash out sin? It is an anxious point. My soul, rest not till you grasp a clear reply. Sin is indeed a hell-dark stain. Wash it with all that nature knows or man can bring, and its black dye becomes more black. If tears of penitence could flow for ever, they would lessen not the frightful shade. The waters from the puddle of man's best resolves leave the stained soul in aggravated stains. Let rivers after rivers of rites and forms and strictest self-denial and most severe observances pass over it, yet still the deeply-grained pollution would be uncleansed. If all angelic hosts could wash the spots with all the innocence of angels' tears, the crimson would be crimson still. And why? Because of sin's intense malignity. Infinity belongs to its polluting touch. Its slightest breath inflicts irreparable soil.

If, then, the Laver would cleanse sin, it must contain a

stream of more than human or angelic power. It must be perfectly divine. It must have all the properties of God. My soul, now view this Laver. It holds a remedy, large as your every need. The blood therein is Jesu's blood – and Jesus is Jehovah's fellow. It must suffice, because its might is vast as He who shed it – and He who shed it is the God-man Jesus.

Your sins, indeed, are many, black and vile. They have all aggravation and all filth. They have been acted and re-acted, in defiance of all light, all conscience, all rebukes, all checks. Their number leaves the sands behind. Their colour makes the night seem fair. But plunge them in these waters. They meet an essence which is infinite to change their hate-ful hue. No speck can now be found. It flees, as night be-fore the face of day. The sin-black soul becomes as white as wool, whiter than the whitest snow.

Satan beholds, and can discern no remnant of a flaw. Nothing is left which he can touch. God looks with an all-searching eye, but sin has fled as far as the east is from the west. It has vanished in the efficacy of this perfect cleans-ing. The blood, the all-powerful blood has washed it out. The Christ-bathed soul is pure and clean and bright and spotless and heaven-fit, even as Christ Himself.

It is so. It must be so. Hear the Spirit's witness. 'The blood of Jesus Christ His Son cleanseth us from all sin.' 1 John 1.7. Lift up the eye. Behold the bright array which throng the throne. Whence is their title to the heavenly home? The blood which bought them has removed all stains. Look down to that dark pit where darkness spreads its ever-darkening pall. Ah! what a spectacle of filth and woe! But wherefore do these wretched spirits writhe in their polluted beds? They never sought, they never found, they never used, the cleansing Laver of a Saviour's blood. Hell holds not one who found it. Unwashed souls must sink. The washed must rise. Vile fetters chain the one. The others mount up with silver wings, and feathers of yellow gold.

But sins forgiven in the court of heaven are not soon forgotten in the court of conscience. Satan finds entrance here. With savage voice and clamorous demand, he drags our bygone acts before its bar. If he cannot cast victims into hell, he will affright the heaven-ward pilgrims with wild storms of fear. Thus he reads out long scrolls of past transgression. He argues that souls so black are only fuel for his endless flames. Woe unto them who strive to reason with this wily foe! Denial cannot be. The case is true. Memory bears tearful witness. Excuses are in vain. These vessels are all full of leaks. They cannot hold defence.

The only refuge is this Laver. They who have Gospel-light will cast themselves therein. Then peace resumes her peaceful reign. Then Satan flees in disappointed rage. Then terrifying threats melt into songs of safety. The adversary yields. He cannot destroy a blood-supported peace.

Reader, would you have conscience an unruffled calm? Would you repose in pastures of heart-ease? Then heal all memory's wounds in this pure Laver. Beside its brink you may securely shout: God is appeased: my troubles shall not live. He sees my sins no more: they are behind His back: they therefore shall not frown before my face.

But the Laver holds more precious water yet. He, who finds Christ finds every good in one. Do you ask: Can more be needed, if sin has lost its filth and guilt? Yes, its vile seeds remain. There is the evil heart bent on all evil. The fire of lust burns strong. The oven of impure desire is hot. But there is water here to purify the will. Christ gives His Holy Spirit to work renewal and to put out sin. What streams of comfort flow in the channel of the Word. 'Then will I sprinkle clean water upon you, and ye shall be clean: from all your filthiness and from all your idols will I cleanse you. A new heart also will I give you, and a new spirit will I put within you: and I will take away the stony heart out of your flesh, and I will give you a heart of flesh.' Ezek. 36.25. 26. The Gospel echoes: He of God is made unto us, not only wisdom and righteousness, but sanctification too. 1 Cor. 1.30.

Reader, has this Laver brought this change to you? Are you a new-made creature in Christ Jesus? Mark well the solemn truth, 'Except a man be born again, he cannot see the kingdom of God.' There is no heaven, but for new-born souls. Insuperable bars shut the old nature out. If title must be found in Christ, so meetness must be got from Him.

But steadily behold the Laver. All is ready here. The blood which buys all pardon, and confers all peace, earns all supplies of sanctifying grace. The constant cry is: Wash and be clean from every outward stain. Wash and be clean from all accusing fears. Wash and be clean from the deep springs of inward evil. Wash and be clean from this world's corrupting love.

The Laver was but one. If Israel's priests had sought some other fount, their case would have been hopeless; the wrath would have consumed them. Reader, cast out the vain conceit that ought but Christ can cleanse the soul. He is enough, He is at hand. But fail to use Him, and your filth remains. Wash here; wash only here. No other vessel can add merit where all merit thus abounds. So only will your walk be clean on earth. So only will you reach the pure abodes where holy lips for ever sing, 'Holy, Holy, Holy, Lord God of hosts.'

THE NAME

*'The Lord passed by before him, and proclaimed, The Lord,
the Lord God, merciful and gracious, long-suffering, and abundant
in goodness and truth, keeping mercy for thousands, forgiving
iniquity and transgression and sin, and that will by no means clear
the guilty.' Exod. 34.6, 7*

Earth owes much to supplicating lips. Abundant harvests
have been reaped from a little seed of interceding grace.
An instance meets us here. A tree of glorious truth rears
its high head. Its wide-spread branches have been refresh-
ing shade to multitudes of every age. But whence its birth?
A hearty prayer was breathed. The noble plant sprang up.

Believer, in every place, and at every time drop seeds
of prayer. The crop may live when your short race
is run.

The suppliant here is Moses. He thirsts for clearer knowledge of his God. He had seen much, and therefore burns
for more. He cries, 'I beseech Thee, show me Thy glory.' It
is a large desire. But gracious souls crave all that God can
give. It is a large petition. But large petitions honour the
Giver and are honoured by Him. Mark the reply. 'I will
make all My goodness pass before thee, and I will proclaim the name of the Lord before thee.' His glory is His
goodness. His goodness is His glory. His name is the page
in which these wonders shine.

Reader, have you this holy wish? Do you long to see this
glory, to taste this goodness, to feast at the banquet of this
knowledge? Come then in faith. Come in the lowliness of
humble awe. The Lord is passing by. He speaks. Heed His
proclaiming voice. 'The Lord, the Lord God, merciful and
gracious, long-suffering, and abundant in goodness and
truth, keeping mercy for thousands, forgiving iniquity and

transgression and sin, and that will by no means clear the guilty.' A train of glory issues from the courts of heaven. Each image shows some glimpse of Him, whose full display would blind our mortal sight.

The foremost in the group utters the name, 'Jehovah.' Oh! wondrous sound! It casts the mind back through the ages of eternity gone by; it bears it forward through eternity to come. It loudly tells that through the past, the present, and the future, One is. It pictures Him as 'I am,' before time was: – 'I am,' when time shall be no more. It robes Him in all the majesty and dignity and grandeur and boundless-ness of changeless unity. It exhibits Him as the sole great fount of every stream of life. O my soul, such is your Lord. Great beyond thought! vast beyond grasp! immeasurable by human line! untraceable by human search! But from this lofty throne His eye was ever fixed on you. Through all infinities, your image filled His heart. His age is immor-tality; He grants the same to you. Will you not adore and reverence and bless Him, and love and praise and serve Him?

'The Lord, the Lord.' Before another sound is heard, Jehovah's name is doubled. The repetition bids us look again. It tells us that thought upon thought must search the mysteries of the great 'I am.' The soaring wing must soar still higher. Our praise must only pause, to recom-mence its endless work.

'The Lord, the Lord God.' The title 'God' is now con-joined. This speaks of power and strength. It claims un-bounded sovereignty. God sits indeed upon a throne omni-potent. He wields the sceptre of unlimited control. His right hand is all power. He speaks, and it must be. He works, and who can hinder? Pile worlds on worlds, His breath can drive them into nothingness. Collect all hosts from earth and hell, His foot can drive the mass to dust.

Shall then poor man vaunt against God? How can a

rebel stand when God shall gird Himself with wrath? Sinner, be wise in time. Vengeance comes on apace. It strides resistless in its force. There is no refuge but at Calvary's cross.

Believer, this name flies down on wings of peace to you. Know the full might, which is your full support. This God is your shield. What foes can harm? He is your sword. Who can assail? He is your fortress. Are you not safe? He is the wall of fire round about you. Who can break through to wound? He has promised life eternal as your portion. Who can prevent? He is bearing you in His own arms to heaven. Who can pluck you from His grasp? This God is your full salvation. Therefore you shall be fully saved.

'The Lord, the Lord God, merciful.' The voice proceeds to open out Jehovah's heart. This heart is mercy. As the sun abounds in sparkling rays, the sea in drops, the sky in glittering orbs, so God is one vast treasure-house of mercy. This is the brightest jewel of His crown. It overtops the heavens. It outlives all time. It outshines all perfections. It is the riches of His riches.

But what is mercy? It is that sweet and tender love which has a tear for all distress, which grieves in grief, and sorrows in sorrow, and yearns over misery, and only lives in healing wounds, and calming anguish, and converting sighs to joy. This looked on man in his lost estate. It marked the present suffering and the future woe. It tarried not. It found a full and perfect remedy, even a God-man's life and death.

The Father is all mercy. A Saviour called, a Saviour sent, a Saviour accepted is the proof. Jesus is all mercy. The manger, the garden, the cross, the blood, the righteousness, the never-ceasing prayer, proclaim it. The Spirit is all mercy. His striving in the heart, His light-diffusing presence, His guidance to the Saviour's arms, His many visits of con soling love, His rich outpourings of renewing grace, bear witness to this truth.

Reader, whatever be your misery, come to this God, and mercy will relieve it. Paul knew the burden of tremendous guilt, but he 'obtained mercy.' The penitent pleaded, 'God, be merciful to me a sinner.' Floods of peace over-flowed. The wretched cried, 'Jesus, thou Son of David, have mercy on me.' Jesus stood still. The answer lingered not. 'Go thy way, thy faith hath made thee whole.' The sorrowing mother supplicated, 'Have mercy on me, O Lord, thou Son of David,' and all relief was given. Mercy still reigns in heaven. Bring then your sins, they shall be pardoned: your tears, they shall be wiped away: your conscience-wounds, they shall be healed: your sighs, they shall be lulled to rest: your need, it shall be all supplied: your difficulties, they shall be smoothed.

'Merciful and gracious.' The view is changed. Another aspect courts the eye. Grace shows its beauteous form. As mercy pities misery, so grace is helpful to unworthiness. Mercy brings balm for wretchedness. Grace hastens to demerit's aid. Mercy finds tender motive in man's woe. Grace has no impulse but from God. The world presents a hateful front. The wide-spread field is rank with mad rebellion's weeds. There is no shame, no penitence, no downcast look, no weeping eye, no sobbing breast, no wringing hand, no prayer for pardon, and no cry for pity. Sin follows sin as wave on wave. But grace springs forth, free as God's freeness, vast as God's vastness. It says, I love because I love. I will save because I will save. I will redeem from hell because I will redeem. It has no cradle but God's own heart. It has no spring but God's own purpose. But it is a worthy offspring of that worthy source. It girds itself to wondrous work. It draws Salvation's plan. It leads forth Salvation's captain. It chooses Salvation's heirs. It consummates Salvation's scheme. It lays the first stone. It adds the top-stone. It cannot rest, until the shout be heard, Grace to it, Grace to it, for ever.

Reader, merit is as far from you as east from west. Your only property is sin. But you may shine in glory, because God is grace. Oh! haste to Him. Take pardon as a free-grace gift. Seek heaven as a free-grace prize. But if your pride rejects free grace, your own deserts will be the undying worm.

'Merciful and gracious, long-suffering.' The citizens of Zion sometimes quake, less grievous guilt should drain all mercy and exhaust all grace. A ray next shines to dissipate these clouds. Behold Me, saith the Lord, I am long-suffering. Here is a plank, on which the wave-tossed soul may rest. What! though the annals of the heart are but a sin-vile tale. What! though each day, each hour, is but the hot-bed of provoking ill. What! though the holiest prayers are often solemn mockery, the holiest works but incense to self-love. Still, vengeance stays the hand, and blessings pour their blessing-showers down. If angels' patience ruled for one hour, would it be so? Nay! Man's whole race would be a shivered ruin. But He who reigns is a long-suffering God. Hence, where offence abounds, His patience rises higher. We live because our God forbears. But the day comes when boundless patience finds its bounds. Sinner, when God's long-suffering can no more bear, then your long sufferings will no more cease.

'Merciful and gracious, long-suffering, and abundant in goodness and truth.' But while patience still is patient, may not the stores of goodness fail? It cannot be. God's goodness is Himself. While He has life, it is His life to scatter goodness round. Believer, come to this tree. Its boughs for ever bend, and all its fruits are goodness. Drink of these waters. They ever flow, and all the stream is goodness. Truth is the handmaid which provides and scatters far these never-failing gifts. A covenant oath is pledged, 'Surely blessing I will bless.' Heb. 6.14. Truth then must die before the hand of goodness can hang down. Abundant truth secures abundant goodness.

'Keeping mercy for thousands.' O my soul, hearken to the melody of this sweet note. The thought may sometimes rise, that mercy visits but a favoured few, that the rare gift enriches but rare souls. Nay, mercy's arms are very wide. Mercy's heart is very large. Mercy's mansions are very many. It has brought saving joy to countless multitudes. It has saving joy for countless yet. The doors stand open. Thousands have found. But there are stores for thousands yet.

Will any hesitate? Will any sigh, There cannot be this hope for me? Whence is the fear? Is the reply, Iniquity forbids? This Name sweeps down such obstacle. It cries, The Lord is a God, 'forgiving iniquity.' Is it added, But transgressions are so vile? The Name still speaks, The Lord is a God forgiving iniquity and transgression. Is it further said, But sins appear in countless multitudes? The Name continues, Our Lord is a God forgiving iniquity and transgression and sin. If all the sins of all the lost, if all the filth of all the fiends in hell, were piled on your one conscience, flee to the cross, plead this sure word, and as our God is true, He will be found forgiving iniquity and transgression and sin.

But if you fail to cast yourself on Christ, there is no other refuge. This word of richest comfort is stern condemnation to all who stand in their own guilt. "He will by no means clear the guilty.' No sinner can take unpardoned sins to heaven. No soul unwashed can enter there. Evil must have what evil earns. Christ our Surety appeared bearing our sins. He was not spared. Wrath seized Him. Vengeance took its due. In Him, all who are His are cleared, because His death is theirs. Out of Him, all who have sin must die, because their sins are theirs.

Reader, such is God's saving Name. Oh! hear it now, and with the ear of faith. It is not heard in hell.

SOME OTHER
BANNER OF TRUTH TRUST
PAPERBACKS

An Alarm to the Unconverted, *Joseph Alleine*, 160 *pages*, 4s 6d

Five Christian Leaders, *J. C. Ryle*, 192 *pages*, 4s 6d

Five Pioneer Missionaries, 352 *pages*, 7s 6d

For a Testimony, *Bruce F. Hunt*, 160 *pages*, 5s

The Forgotten Spurgeon, *Iain Murray*, 224 *pages*, 5s

Genesis 3, *E. J. Young*, 176 *pages*, 5s

*God-Centred Evangelism, *R. B. Kuiper*, 240 *pages*, 6s

The Gospel in Genesis, *Henry Law*, 192 *pages*, 3s

John Bunyan, *Frank Harrison*, 232 *pages*, 5s

Letters of John Newton, 192 *pages*, 4s 6d

The Life of Elijah, *A. W. Pink*, 320 *pages*, 6s

The Life of M'Cheyne, *Andrew Bonar*, 192 *pages*, 3s 6d

Prayer, *John Bunyan*, 176 *pages*, 4s 6d

The Rare Jewel of Christian Contentment, *Jeremiah Burroughs*, 240 *pages*, 4s 6d

*Redemption Accomplished and Applied, *John Murray*, 192 *pages*, 3s

*Roman Catholicism, *Loraine Boettner*, 560 *pages*, 8s 6d

Sermons of George Whitefield, 192 *pages*, 4s 6d

The Sovereignty of God, *A. W. Pink*, 160 *pages*, 2s 6d

*A Summary of Christian Doctrine, *Louis Berkhof*, 192 *pages*, 3s 6d

Unity in the Dark, *Donald Gillies*, 128 *pages*, 3s 6d

* *Not for sale in USA or Canada.*